Fishing New England

A Rhode Island Shore Guide

About the Author

Gene Bourque, editor of *On The Water* magazine, grew up in Mystic, Connecticut, and learned to fish in the waters of southeastern Connecticut and along the South County beaches of Rhode Island. After moving to Cape Cod in 1973, he worked in local tackle shops and began fishing the Cape from the Canal to Provincetown. He has been a shore guide, teaches fly-fishing and fly-tying and gives seminars for fishing clubs and at sporting shows throughout the Northeast.

Fishing New England
A Rhode Island Shore Guide

Gene Bourque

Joanne Briana-Gartner

with additional text by
Joe Lyons
Dave Pickering
Charley Soares

On The Water
Falmouth, MA

Printed in the United States of America

Library of Congress Card Number: 2001095532

ISBN # 0-9706538-1-6

10 9 8 7 6 5 4 3 2 1

Book design and cover photograph by Joanne Briana-Gartner
Interior photographs by: Gene Bourque, Joanne Briana-Gartner
and Peg Verdi

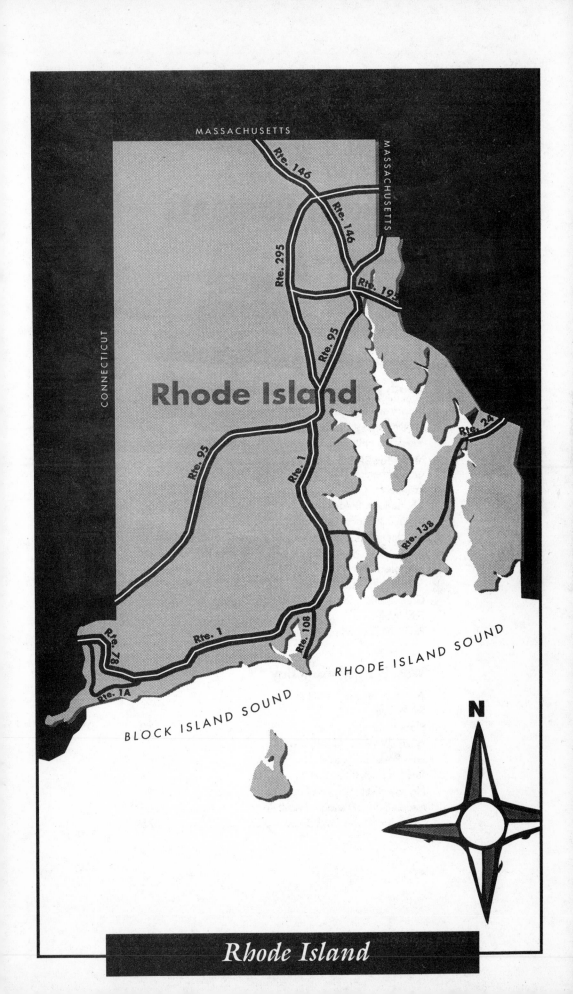

Rhode Island

Table of Contents

Table of Contents

Acknowledgements

This book could not have been possible without the assistance of an outstanding group of Rhode Island anglers. Writers, tackle shop owners and employees, charter captains and guides, and everyday fishermen, these folks know and love fishing the rocky shores and beaches of the Ocean State. They are all experts, and their willingness to share their knowledge and insights is greatly appreciated. This group includes, in no particular order, Dave Pickering, Joe Lyons, Charley Soares, Dave Souza, Joe Martins, Steve Cook, Andy Dangelo, Justin Civic, Ron Mouchon, Cindy Swan, Cory Pietraszek and Ladd Meyer.

Introduction

Growing up in Mystic, Connecticut, it was only a short ride to the beaches of the South Shore of Rhode Island. My first realization that fishing was more than lowering a drop line off a dock for flatfish (flounder) came one foggy morning at Weekapaug, Rhode Island. I was probably about ten years old and my family had arrived early for a day on the beach. The fog was supposed to burn off later, but it was pea soup thick as we walked down toward some favorite sand dunes and the swells swept in and broke close to the shore.

Out of the fog came a figure in waders, a plug bag slung over his shoulder, the longest fishing rod I'd ever seen in one hand and the other hand under the gill plate of a huge fish that he dragged along the beach. I know now that it must have been a striper that was well over 20 pounds, a relatively common catch in those days, but to me it seemed incredible that such a monster could be in the same waters in which I was about swim.

As I remember it, my Dad complimented the fisherman on his catch and asked where the fish was caught, but the angler just mumbled something about "down the beach" and continued on his way, disappearing into the fog. To my young eyes, this was a whole new world of fishing that I had imagined only existed in the faraway locales I'd seen on *American Sportsman* on television and in magazines. The heavy tackle and of course the fish made an immediate impression, but so did the fisherman's demeanor, which spoke to me of a man versus the elements, contesting a foe that could not easily be defeated. What ten-year-old wouldn't be impressed?

This phantom fisherman was one of the legion of Rhode Island surfcasters and shore fishermen who have enjoyed the fantastic and varied fishing opportunities in the Ocean State for generations. In fact, the sportfishing tradition goes back well over 150 years, dating back to the West Island Club, an exclusive retreat off Little Compton, founded by millionaires from Newport and the predecessor of the famous Cuttyhunk Bass Club. Right after the end of World War II, returning GIs began driving surplus jeeps along the beaches of South County in search of striped bass. They formed fishing clubs, many of which are active today.

Little Rhody may be the smallest state but it has 384 miles of tidal shoreline, offering just about every type of saltwater fishing experience, from oceanfront sandy beaches where large summer flounder can be caught, to rocky points and outcroppings that are striped bass and bluefish magnets, to estuary systems and marshes that attract weakfish (squeteague) and stripers.

As compared to fishermen in more northerly New England states, Rhode Island shore anglers have to be a little more resourceful, a little more committed to losing sleep and a little more willing to take advantage of opportunities that present themselves.

On Cape Cod, the north shore of Massachusetts and on up into New Hampshire and southern Maine, striper and bluefish anglers have the luxury of a fishery that for most part is consistent throughout the season. The fish may arrive later, but they stay close by and in many cases can be caught in the daylight on all but the hottest days of summer.

Not so in the Ocean State. The bulk of the migratory striped bass and bluefish pass by Rhode Island on their way to points north. The water close to shore is just too warm from late June through early September. Out on the reefs and in the deep water near Block Island, Rhode Island boat fishermen take big fish all season, but those who must fish from shore have to become night owls if they want to take home a big striper in the summer. Schools of marauding bluefish swing in close to the shorefront during the day in the summer, but the pre-dawn hours are best for bass.

This is not to say that Rhode Island fishermen have nothing to fish for in the summer—far from it. In fact, they have some opportunities that anglers from the northern states only wish they had. The most glamorous of these may be the chance to take a bonito or false albacore from the shore. In the summer and fall, these speedsters roam up and down the south coast and into Narragansett Bay. Light-tackle enthusiasts and fly-fishermen look for them at the breachways, along the shores of Point Judith, around Aquidneck Island and the eastern shore of the Bay.

Ocean State anglers also have a good shot at weakfish (squeteague) in the spring and after dark through the summer and fall. These fish have been making a modest comeback in the last few years, after virtually disappearing for the last two decades. The beaches of South County are also a great place to fish for fluke (summer flounder). This is another species that has made a comeback, but in this case, the comeback has been much more dramatic. It is quite possible to "limit out" on these delicious fish along any of the sandy-bottomed South County beaches.

It is a virtual certainty that dropping a small piece of squid on a small hook into ten feet or so of water anywhere in the outer Bay will produce all the scup you can handle. These scrappy little fish are a great way to introduce a youngster to the joys of fishing and they are quite tasty, too. Be sure to check the up-to-date bag limit and size regulations, as these fish tend to run small, but their fun factor far outweighs their size. In fact, there are so many of them in Rhode Island waters that they have become a major part of the state's commercial fishery.

For the hardcore shore fishermen, though, striped bass and bluefish are the main focus. After September 15 anglers cruise the beaches of South County in Westerly and Charlestown in four-wheel-drive vehicles in search of blitzing bass and blues. These beaches and the rocky points of Little Compton, Point Judith, Aquidneck Island and Conanicut Island, and Watch Hill are favorite locations not only of local anglers, but of anglers from the north who follow the striper and bluefish migration south. In fact, it is often possible to take large stripers off the beaches of Westerly into December.

It's then just a few cold months until the first schoolies are caught at the West Wall or Matunuck, usually by the last week of April. Over those months, Rhode Island fishermen stay busy with the many active surf-casting, fly-fishing and beach buggy club functions and seminars. This helps to get through those dark months, but it also reaffirms the social aspects of fishing in the Ocean State, something that has always been part of the experience here. Spend an evening fishing at Charlestown Breachway and it will seem that everyone with a rod in his hand knows the guy fishing next to him. This is one of the signs of a great fishing area: a long-standing tradition of camaraderie. You'll see it at Montauk, New York, and Race Point on Cape Cod, and you'll see it at many of the fine fishing spots in Rhode Island.

The locations selected for inclusion in this book were chosen for both the dedicated surf-fishing enthusiast and the casual weekend angler. Some of them are docks, piers or jetties that are appropriate for youngsters, elderly or handicapped fishermen who seek a safe spot to spend the day and have a reasonable chance of catching dinner. Some require effort to fish, and safety equipment, such as studded footwear, is a must. In all cases, it is possible to drive to and park near the location. This was also a requirement for inclusion, and for this reason some Rhode Island locations, such as Block Island and Prudence Island, both of which have very good shore fishing but require a ferry ride to get there, were not included.

It is hoped that *Fishing New England, A Rhode Island Shore Guide* will be a starting point to finding some great fishing. But remember, for every location included in this book, there are probably a dozen more that the curious and energetic angler can discover on his or her own.

Gene Bourque

Daytime bait fishermen often prop their rods up in the rocks at the East Wall.

Camping

An inexpensive option for the shore angler who wants to spend time close to some great fishing spots without breaking the bank is to stay at one of two State of Rhode Island camping areas in South County. At one area, Burlingame State Park, you don't even need a tent! These parks are administered by the Rhode Island Division of Environmental Management, Department of Parks and Recreation.

Burlingame State Park, Charlestown
This park is off Route 1 in Charlestown. Burlingame is a short drive from Quanochontaug Breachway, East Beach, Charlestown Breachway and Matunuck. The park covers 2,100 acres, with picnic and recreation areas and swimming in a pond with lifeguards on duty in the summer. There are 755 campsites for tents or RVs, available on a "first come, first served" basis without reservations. There are also six "camping cabins" available by reservation. These cabins are a great value, and hot showers, flush toilets and a camp store are nearby. They are reserved quickly each season, especially on and around holidays.

Cabin reservation forms (required) are available by sending a self-addressed, stamped envelope to: Burlingame State Park, 1 Burlingame State Park, Charlestown, RI 02813; or they can be downloaded online at www.riparks.com/cabin.htm. The camping area operates from April 15 through October 31. For further information call 401-322-7337.

Fishermen's Memorial State Park and Campground, Narragansett
From the junction of Route 1 and Route 108, follow Route 108 south for 4 miles to the park entrance on the right.
This campground is smaller than Burlingame but is even closer to some great fishing in the Point Judith area. There are 182 sites here, available by reservation (five-night minimum) or "first come, first served" on a per-night basis. Three state beaches are nearby for families with non-fishing members, and the Point Judith ferry to Block Island is just one mile away. The campground, with full facilities, including showers, flush toilets and hookups for RVs, is open from April 15 through October 31. Camping is available, with limited facilities, from November 1 through 14 for fishermen wishing to take advantage of the great late-season striper fishing on Point Judith. This campground has plenty of open space and large sites with hookups that are preferred by RV fans.

For a (required) reservation form, write to Fisherman's Memorial Park and Campground, 1011 Point Judith Road, Narragansett, RI 02882 or download the form from the Web site: www.riparks.com/fisherma.htm. For more information call 401-789-8374.

There are also dozens of private campgrounds close to the fishing areas listed in this book. Brochures for these campgrounds are available at many roadside tourist information booths around the state or through local chambers of commerce.

This fisherman works the surf from the rocks at the south end of Scarborough Beach.

Access, Regulations and Your Rights

Information contained in this book about access to fishing locations and parking is accurate and current at the date of publication, but keep in mind that these rules and regulations may change on a yearly or seasonal basis. In some communities, such as the resorts of Watch Hill and Newport, parking regulations are vigorously enforced year-round.

Federal and state laws guarantee access to the water, but you may not cross private property to get there. In other words, you are within your rights to fish anywhere on the shore of Rhode Island below the mean high water line, even in front of a multi-million dollar mansion, but you must not cross the lawn in front of the mansion to do so (unless the owner happens to be a fisherman himself and gives you permission).

Fortunately, there is plenty of information available about the locations profiled in this book and many others that you may want to explore. Two Internet Web sites that are particularly helpful are:

www.riparks.com

Posted by the State of Rhode Island, Department of Environmental Management (DEM), Division of Parks and Recreation, this site lists all the state parks and state camping areas. Information is provided on access, fees and regulations; directions, telephone numbers and links to special events are listed; a tide chart and hurricane watch are provided; and even information on water quality and ozone conditions are available.

http://seagrant.gso.uri.edu/riseagrant/ AccessGuide/environmental_guide.html
This is the online version of a wonderful book published in 1993 but now out of print, *Public Access to the Rhode Island Coast* by Pamela Pogue and Virginia Lee. This book is now entirely available via the Internet. Published by the Rhode Island Sea Grant Advisory Service, it lists hundreds of well-known and obscure access points to the coast, with written descriptions of each. Also included are lists of services, the type of environment found at each spot (rocky beach, sandy beach, marsh, etc.) and popular uses.

If you would like your own copy of the book, a limited number of copies are available for $10, plus $2.50 shipping and handling from:

Rhode Island Sea Grant Publications Office
University of Rhode Island
Narragansett Bay Campus
Narragansett, RI 02882

The Department of Environmental Management, Division of Fisheries and Wildlife maintains over 100 fishermen's access areas, boat ramps and other public facilities throughout the state. Much of the information about these areas is available at the www.riparks.com Web site, but up-to-the-minute information about access to specific sites is available through the Great Swamp Field Headquarters (401-789-0281) or through the DEM Enforcement Office (401-222-3070).

Fishing New England
A Rhode Island Shore Guide

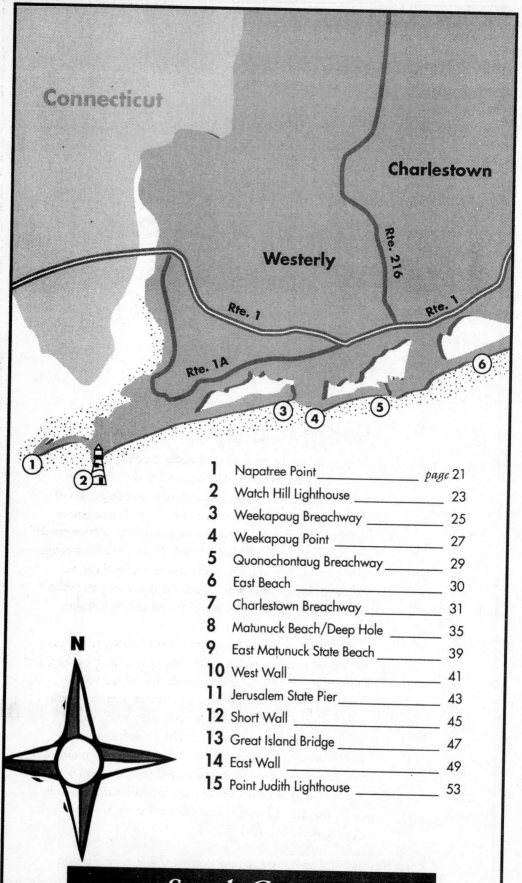

South County

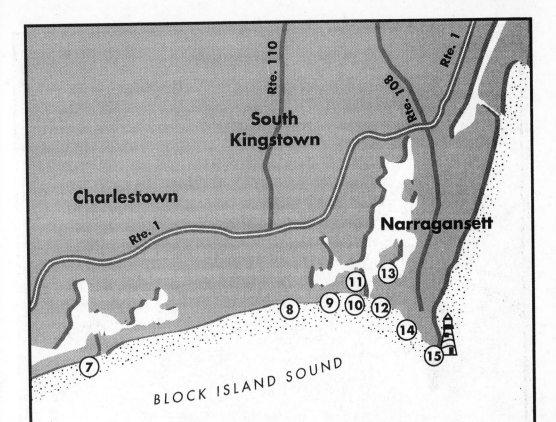

South County

Known throughout the state as **South County**, the stretch from the West Wall in Galilee, west to Watch Hill and the border of Connecticut, is a shoreline of alternating areas of sandy barrier beach and rocky points. Behind these barrier beaches are large salt ponds, and the openings to these ponds are known as the breachways: Weekapaug, Quonochontaug, Charlestown and the opening of Point Judith Pond into the Harbor of Refuge at Galilee. Just about every saltwater fisherman in Rhode Island fishes one of the breachways at some point in the season.

Although access to the beach areas has become increasingly problematic in recent years with rising property values, many of the small summer beach colonies still seem like working-class vacation getaways, in contrast to many of the shorefront communities in neighboring Connecticut and Massachusetts. There is also access by four-wheel drive to certain beaches in Westerly and Charlestown in the spring and fall. Many fishermen take advantage of this, cruising the beachfronts in search of stripers and bluefish and using their beach buggies as bases of operation to fish the breachways for days or weeks at a time.

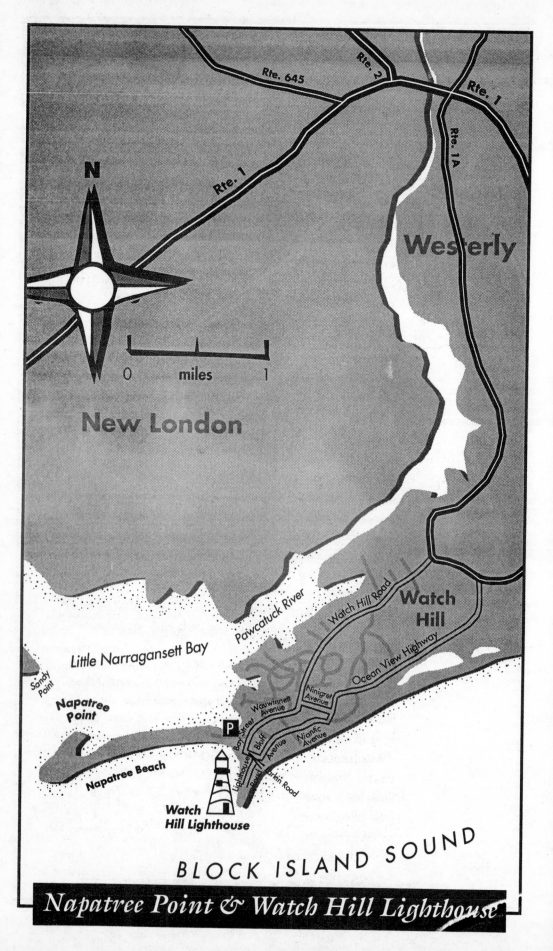

Napatree Point, Watch Hill

Directions:

From the junction of Route 1 and Route 1A in Westerly center, follow Route 1A south 3 1/2 miles to Watch Hill Road. Follow Watch Hill Road southwest 1 1/2 miles, then take a right onto Bay Street, to the municipal parking area.

The 1 1/4-mile strand of beach leading out to **Napatree Point** is well known and an extremely productive location for the shore angler. Before the great hurricane of 1938, a cottage community sat here, and a paved road led out to the point where there was a small fort, part of a string of coastal defenses built in the late nineteenth century. The hurricane utterly destroyed the houses on the isthmus, along with the paved road out to the fort. It also separated the southwestern arm of the point from the mainland, and gradually a sand bar island formed, called Sandy Point, which is now officially part of nearby Connecticut. The water off the northern shore of Napatree, around Sandy Point, and the area at the mouth of the Pawcatuck River are known as Little Narragansett Bay.

Today all that remains of the fort are some crumbling, graffiti-covered concrete gun emplacements, overgrown with poison ivy, low shrubs and weeds. But the rocky shore below the old fort, along with nearby Watch Hill reef, are the eastern terminus of what has become known as the Fishers Island/Watch Hill reef complex and is a favorite spot to look for stripers and bluefish. Swirling tidal currents, a prevailing southwest breeze, ocean swells crashing on the rocks and the influence of the flow from the Pawcatuck River combine to create an environment that attracts bait and sportfish.

The rocks around the point are best fished with relatively heavy surf-casting gear and surface plugs, but it's usually possible to find a lee side to bait fish. Fly-fishermen like either side of the long sandy beach out to the point. Bluefish and sometimes bonito and false albacore can be taken close to shore, especially on the north side of the point.

The Storm of the Century

There are no trees along Napatree Point. The trees, along with the tall grass that lined this barrier beach in Colonial times, were washed away during the 1815 Great Gale. It would be 123 years until the next major hurricane, the infamous Hurricane of 1938, struck New England.

At the time of the hurricane, Napatree Point was serving as Watch Hill's bathing beach, complete with beach club, bathing pavilion and bathhouse all located at Napatree's eastern end. Fort Road, named for Fort Mansfield, an abandoned artillery post on Napatree's western point, ran for roughly one mile, and was lined with 33 summer cottages. The ruins of Fort Mansfield are still evident today; however, no evidence of the cottages exists. The cottages, and all 42 people in them at the time, were swept into and across the sheltered water behind the barrier beach, known as Little Narragansett Bay. Fifteen were drowned. The survivors, clinging to wreck-

Fish can be found anywhere along the beach leading out to Napatree Point.

age, were carried the two miles across the bay, landing on the Connecticut shore, most of them around Osbrook Point by the Pawcatuck River.

When the massive storm surge came in, a man who observed the incoming tidal wave from Watch Hill said that he saw it "covering everything on Fort Road like a long roll of cotton." The wind meter at Watch Hill Coast Guard Station recorded the gust that rendered it inoperative: 120 miles per hour. That was far from peak, though, and no one knows for sure how hard the wind blew that day. It has never blown that hard since.

The hurricane happened upon Napatree Point so fast that only five people were able to escape by car before the first houses washed away. The storm had the element of surprise in its favor. In 1938 there was no Weather Channel with blow-by-blow hype/analysis, no satellite tracking, no computer models, no hurricane hunter reconnaissance. The Weather Bureau (as it was then known) relied on ships at sea to supply whatever meteorological data they could.

On September 21, 1938, at 9 A.M. the Weather Bureau received a report that the storm's location was roughly 100 miles east of Cape Hatteras, North Carolina. After that, according to Dr. James Kimball of the Weather Bureau's New York office, they received "not a scrap of information." From this report until shortly before landfall on eastern Long Island only six hours later, the Bureau was in the blind. By around 3:30 P.M. the first cottages were slipping into the sea at Napatree.

Still, there were those who instinctively knew something was amiss. Though the stripers were said to be running strong off Block Island, the Portuguese-American fishermen from nearby Stonington, Connecticut, decided to stay in port because they did not like the previous evening's copper-colored sunset. No doubt their lives were saved by their keen "fisherman's instinct."

J. Lyons

Watch Hill Lighthouse, Watch Hill

Looking south, you'll see Napatree Point and Watch Hill Reef.

Directions:

From the junction of Route 1 and Route 1A in Westerly center, follow Route 1A south 3 1/2 miles to Watch Hill Road. Follow Watch Hill Road southwest 1 1/2 miles, then take a right onto Bay Street to the municipal parking area. Walk up Larkin Road toward the top of the hill, then down Lighthouse Road on the right.

A Special Note Regarding Parking in Watch Hill:

In the summer, parking in the downtown business area of Watch Hill is very difficult and restrictive, and parking on the side streets is impossible without a

Just offshore from the lighthouse is Watch Hill Reef, one of the premier boat fishing locations in the Ocean State. Striped bass, bluefish, fluke, bonito and false albacore are caught here, and if the reef is fishing well, it's a good bet that the rocks around the **Watch Hill Lighthouse** will, too. This is another location where great care should be taken traversing and fishing from the seaweed-covered rocks. Watch Hill is about the westernmost point on the southern New England shore that feels the full impact of Atlantic Ocean swells, which makes for some spectacular whitewater fishing, but it is also dangerous. Though the best fishing takes place here after dark and at first light, scouting the spot in the day is essential.

If the waves don't allow fishing on the southern or eastern part of the point, try fishing over the grass and rock patches on the west side. Big stripers sometimes seek out the relatively calm waters here and will take a live eel or surface-swimming plug, fished very slowly, in the dark of night. This is a good place to pick up some big blackfish, too.

To the east of the point, the shoreline curves to the east and changes from large boulders to sandy beach. This beach is filled with bathers by day in the summer, but in the evening and early morning it's a great place to look for bluefish, stripers and fluke very close to shore.

Surfcaster's Heaven

I can tell you that eels and surface swimmers are good choices for nocturnal surfcasters plying the waters of Watch Hill Light during the new moons of June and October. I can tell you that poppers and metal are a smart pick when a high tide corresponds with a gray dawn in November, or that rainy

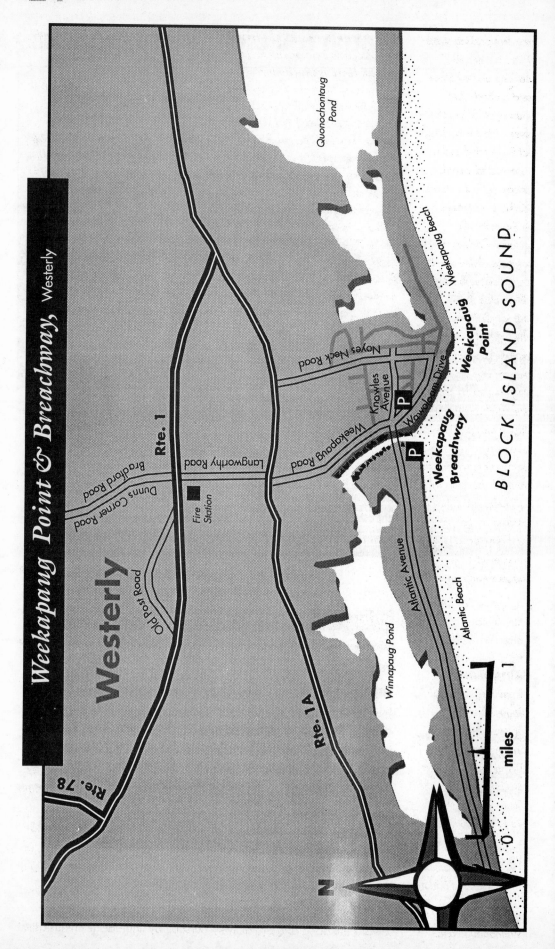

Weekapaug Point & Breachways, Westerly

Westerly

Rte. 78

Rte. 1

Old Post Road

Bradford Road

Dunns Corner Road

Langworthy Road

Fire Station

Rte. 1A

Winnapaug Pond

Noyes Neck Road

Knowles Avenue

Weekapaug Road

Wawaloam Drive

P

P

Weekapaug Breachway

Atlantic Avenue

Atlantic Beach

Quonochontaug Pond

Weekapaug Beach

Weekapaug Point

BLOCK ISLAND SOUND

N

0   1   miles

resident parking sticker. There is metered parking on Bay Street and a good-sized municipal lot just off the street, but this parking lot is guarded and is reserved for people shopping in the stores. Parking restrictions are enthusiastically enforced, tickets are very expensive and tow trucks patrol the streets. If you plan to fish Napatree Point or near the lighthouse in the summer, be sure to feed the parking meters regularly or be out of the municipal lot before the stores open. The situation loosens up somewhat in the spring and fall, but cars will still be towed if they are parked on side streets that are posted resident-only, even if they appear to be deserted.

September afternoons, the first day of a tropical front, can be red hot. But somehow imparting just the technical leaves the story vastly untold; there is much more going on here than just fishing.

You may hear that at certain places surfcasting takes on significance beyond mere recreation, or that, at such places, the rewards transcend catching fish. You may have even heard that for some, surfcasting borders on a religious experience. If for you surfcasting is somehow spiritual, welcome to one of its cathedrals. If, on the other hand, you do not believe in such things, if you are one of those people for whom success must be measurable or quantifiable, maybe you have picked the wrong pastime.

For if ever there was a place that encompassed surfcasting's underlying themes of personal quest and mysticism, it is Watch Hill Light. Whether it be the perpetual struggle between sea and shore that we feel each time a fish pulls its way and we pull ours; or the understanding of, and connection to, a surfcasting legacy stretching back to the inception of the sport; those surfcasting experiences, along with other more elusive and individual ones, can also be found here.

Watch Hill has all the elements that make surfcasting great. The camaraderie of an early morning blitz with a host of capable anglers; the solitude of a late-night, midweek eel-slingers watch; the forlorn success of one who capitalizes on early December's last migratory fish. The real alongside the imagined, the apparent along with the indescribable, all lie somewhere under Watch Hill's beacon. With every revolution of the light, that which is undefinable comes closer to being revealed.

Far off your right shoulder, a forest of surf rods gathers at Montauk Point; over your left and out to sea, just over the horizon, lies Block Island. You are at Watch Hill, somewhere between these two distinct cultures. Watch Hill is sometimes crowded, sometimes vacant, always promising.

J. Lyons

Weekapaug Breachway, Westerly

Directions:
From the junction of Route 78 and Route 1, go east 2.1 miles to Langworthy Road. Travel south 0.6 miles on Langworthy Road to Route 1A, west 100 yards on Route 1A, then south 0.8 miles on Weekapaug Road to the parking areas on either side of the bridge spanning the outlet to Winnapaug Pond.

Westernmost of the four breachways, which are famous among Rhode Island fishermen, **Weekapaug Breachway** is generally considered the least productive but is still popular, particularly in the early and late season with the bait-slinging crowd. The prime casting positions at the end of either side only have room for a few fishermen, and the experienced hands will rotate positions as fish are hooked and landed. A live or chunk bait drifted out with the dropping tide under a big bobber is a popular method here.

If the prime spots on the jetty are taken, it is still possible to find some good stripers, bluefish or fluke off the beaches on either side of the breachway, but these beaches are popular, so fishing is best done in the pre-dawn hours or in the dark of night. In September, schools of false albacore sometimes charge into the entrance and on up toward the pond and are actively pursued by light-tackle enthusiasts.

Cast and retrieve close to the rocks at the end of Weekapaug Breachway.

Be aware that the rocks on the outer portion of the jetties are awash in crashing ocean swells at times, particularly when strong offshore storms pass in the fall, so appropriate footwear is essential.

Access to the breachway and the adjacent beaches was secured after many years of work by local anglers and fishing clubs. It's important to be courteous and never leave trash, discarded fishing line or empty bait boxes here to ensure continued access to this area.

Rotation at Jetty's End

The best spot to fish on Rhode Island's South County breachways is at the end of the jetties where the outflows meet the sea. Most experienced fishermen know this and often set up a traffic jam at the end of the jetty. To make for organized fishing, many fishermen will fish these areas in rotation.

Here's how it works. The fisherman nearest the outflow casts first and free-spools his offering. He then steps aside and the next person casts and does the same routine. It continues this way for up for up to a half-dozen fishermen. When it's working right, the first fisherman should be retrieving his lure and then walking to the front of the line as the last fisherman has cast. The rotation is ready to begin again.

Etiquette dictates that you should always ask fishermen already at the end of the jetty if they want to fish in rotation, and everyone should reel in their lines if someone hooks a fish.

D. Pickering

Weekapaug Point, Westerly

The rocks along Weekapaug Breachway hold stripers, especially when the surf is up.

Directions:

From the junction of Route 78 and Route 1, go east 2.1 miles to Langworthy Road. Travel south 0.6 miles on Langworthy Road to Route 1A. Go west 100 yards on Route 1A, then south 0.8 miles on Weekapaug Road to the junction of Weekapaug Road, Knowles Avenue, Atlantic Avenue and Wawoloam Drive. Proceed straight through this intersection onto Wawoloam Drive and follow it in a southeasterly direction for 0.6 mile to the designated parking sites on the street.

East of Weekapaug Breachway is a small beach and the beginning of a quarter-mile stretch of rocky shoreline that holds striped bass and bluefish. **Weekapaug Point** is a place for relatively heavy surf-casting gear and surface plugs, although some anglers score well here with live eels cast and retrieved at night. The difficulty is finding a safe spot among the boulders to approach the water. Be sure to have a game plan in place for landing fish, too. This spot is dangerous when a large swell is running, so much so that many locals come here just to watch nature's show when the surf is up. But these conditions draw in the stripers too, so if the ocean has settled down after a strong southwest or southeast blow, look for some trophy fish to be among the rocks just off shore.

Spicing Up A Jig

Bucktail jigs are very effective for spring and fall schoolies and will take an occasional squeteague. They can be spiced up in a number of ways for even greater effectiveness. Many fishermen in the past, as well as some today, will add pork rind strips for a fluttering tail. More popular these days are grub tails, or plastic curly tails, in various lengths and colors. These tails, when threaded on the jig's hook, swim back and forth quickly and enticingly. Other fishermen thread plastic worms onto their jigs, especially in the spring when seaworms may be swarming. Another trick is to add a teaser ahead of your jig. The teaser can be a fly, a commercially produced Red Gill or even a plain curly tail threaded onto a hook. All of these extras make a big difference when fishing a bucktail jig.

D. Pickering

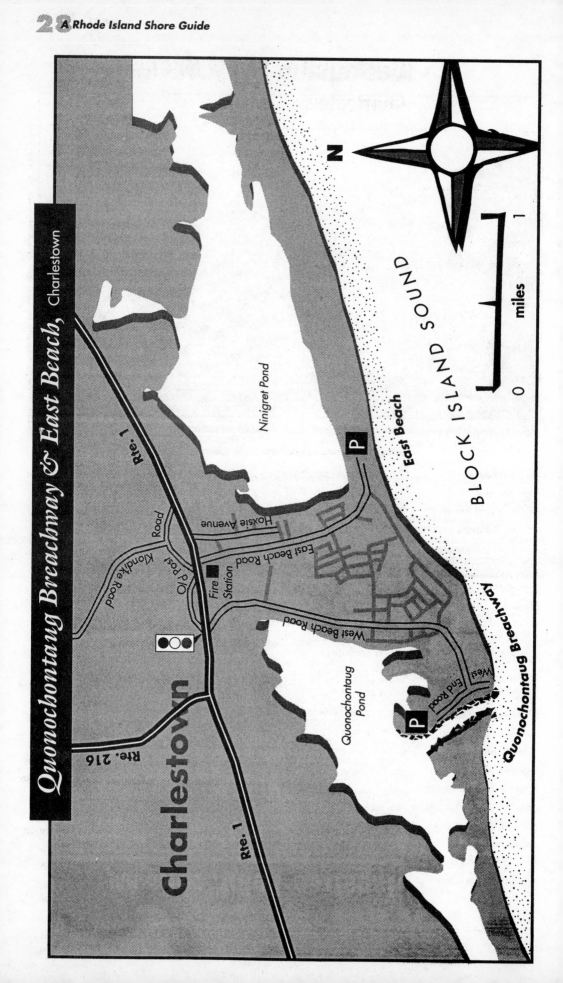

Quonochontaug Breachway & East Beach, Charlestown

N

1

miles

0

BLOCK ISLAND SOUND

East Beach

Ninigret Pond

P

Hoxsie Avenue

East Beach Road

Old Post Road

Klondike Road

Fire Station

Rte. 1

West Beach Road

Quonochontaug Pond

West End Road

P

Quonochontaug Breachway

Charlestown

Rte. 216

Rte. 1

Quonochontaug Breachway,
Charlestown

A strong ripline forms off the end of Quonny Breachway.

Directions:

From Route 1 in Charlestown, follow West Beach Road south 1 1/2 miles, then west 1/2 mile to West End Road. Turn right onto West End road and follow 1/8 mile to the parking area at the public boat ramp.

"Quonny" Breachway is a bit more difficult to approach on foot than the other two breachways, but it's worth the effort. The angler must either walk the rocks along the breachway to the end on the east side or make the mile-plus walk from the parking lot at East Beach. This is because all the property close by the beach end of the breachway is private and no one is allowed to cross. There is a gated access point between the houses on the south end of West End Road, but this gate is often locked. Once the fisherman gains the end of the jetty, he'll find a classic rip on an outgoing tide where a chunk bait drifted out under a bobber, or a live eel drifted after dark, can produce a good striper.

On an incoming tide, try the fast water of the breachway itself or the deeper water near the ramp with swimming plugs. Fly-fishermen often do well after dark, wading the edges of Quonochontaug Pond near the breachway.

In the off season, when the summer beach houses are boarded up, it is easier to gain access to the outer beach.

Free-Spooling Surface Swimmers

One of the best lures to use at the Rhode Island South County breachways at night on the outgoing tides is a large surface swimmer or a Danny-style swimmer. These swimmers are cast way out in the outgoing currents and then free-spooled for greater distance. Once the desired distance is reached, the reel is locked into gear and the plug is simply held in the current. The plug's movement can be felt by the pulsating rod tip as the current imparts action. When the plug swings out of the current and no tip action is felt, retrieve it slowly. This technique accounts for many big bass and blues in the breachways, especially on fall nights.

D. Pickering

At the end of the breachway you can look toward Quonochontaug Pond.

East Beach, Charlestown

Directions:

From Route 1, drive south for 1 mile, then east 1/4 mile on East Road to the state beach parking area.

This beautiful three-mile beach is popular with the off-road-vehicle fishing crowd. There is a sand trail on the back of the barrier beach leading to a designated camping area for four-wheelers. In the fall, after the shore bird nesting season, the outer beach is opened to vehicles, and fishermen keep an eye out for blitzing bluefish and bass, especially when there is a strong onshore wind blowing, combined with an ocean swell.

Working west from the parking area, there are plenty of rocky outcroppings and structure just off **East Beach** all the way to Quonny Breachway. This is a good hike, but there is plenty of fishy water here that should be explored thoroughly. The best-known structure along this part of the beach is known as the Fresh Pond Rocks. This area fishes best at the middle stages of the tide when white water forms among the rocks, but there is still enough depth to keep lures from getting hung up. Although many people fish the edges of this rock pile out of fear of losing gear, many fish are taken by experienced regulars among the rocks. A live eel, unweighted, worked around these rocks can be deadly. Be sure to use heavy gear here to turn the big fish away from the boulders.

East Beach is a great spot to fish live bait or to cast plugs.

Riding the Beach, 4X4 Adventure

For those looking to ride the sands and fish from the beach, East Beach is the place to be. After September 15, fishermen who obtain the required permits may ride the beach at East Beach and reach some faraway spots to the north of the parking area. Permits may be purchased at the office at Burlingame State Park off Route 1.

Besides the permit, other safety devices must be on board any vehicle that is on the beach. These include a shovel, tow rope or chain, jack, support stand, spare tire, tire gauge, first aid kit, fire extinguisher, appropriate emergency signal devices and/or a two-way radio or cell phone, and a flashlight. And, of course, don't forget your fishing gear!

D. Pickering

Charlestown Breachway,
Charlestown

Directions:

From Route 1 in Charlestown, proceed south 0.3 mile on Narrow Lane to Matunuck School House Road. Follow Matunuck School House Road east for 0.1 mile to Charlestown Beach Road on the right. Follow Charlestown

This is the most popular and famous of the breachways, and for good reason. Large stripers are taken off the **Charlestown Breachway** all season, although in the summer it is best fished after dark. In the fall the beach parking lot is filled with buggies bristling with surf rods. Many Rhody anglers plan their vacations every year around the fall run of striped bass and bluefish here, camping at nearby Burlingame State Park or near the breachway itself.

All popular surf-casting methods work here, including plug casting, drifting chunk baits and casting live eels. The outgoing tide is best and here, as at all the breachways, a system of fishing etiquette is practiced by the experienced regulars. When a fish is hooked by the angler at the end of the jetty, he shouts out, "Fish on!" and the other anglers pull in lines and allow him to pass and make his way to

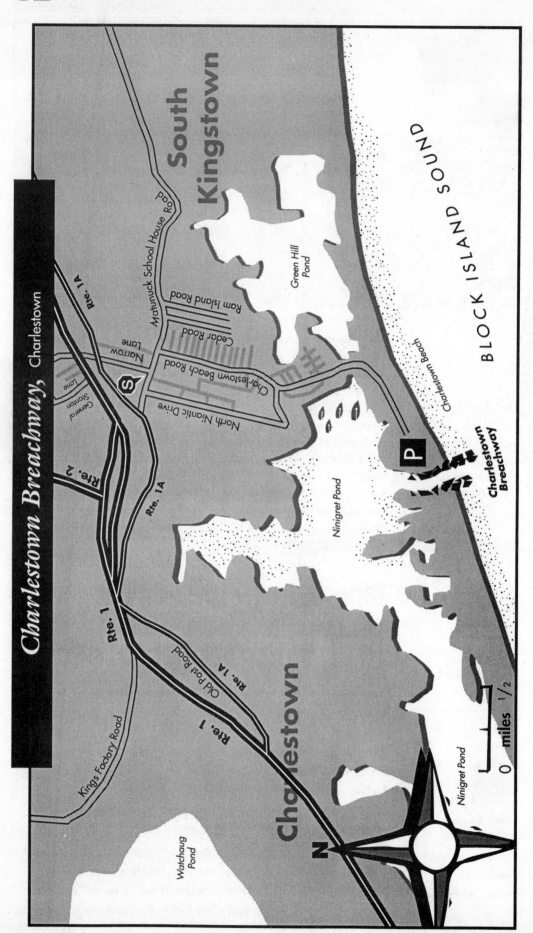

Charlestown Breachway, Charlestown

Beach Road south 1.3 miles, then west 0.5 mile to the town beach parking and camping area.

the beach where he'll fight and hopefully land his fish. The angler closest to the end of the jetty then takes the preferred position at the end, all others move up a position and the process starts again. If conditions are very crowded, this rotation system may be used for every cast, regardless of whether a fish is hooked or not. And woe be to the uninitiated or ignorant fisherman who tries to muscle in on a prime position when it isn't his turn!

Keep in mind the tidal flow out of the breachways doesn't start until two to three hours after the high tide on the outside beaches because the huge salt ponds behind the barrier beaches must fill before the flow can reverse.

Of interest to light-tackle and fly-fishermen are the yearly worm spawning swarms in Ninigret Pond. The breachway is the flushing mechanism for this huge salt pond and every spring when the water inside reaches about 60 degrees, a species of saltwater worm emerges from the soft bottom by the thousands and the stripers seem to

An angler can look into Ninigret Pond from the Charlestown Breachway.

know when this event will take place. Small red or brown streamer flies or slim, small rubber baits, rigged without weight, will catch the stripers, which can go on feeding binges that must be seen to be believed. Although most of the bass feeding on the worms will be the schoolie variety, every year a few in the 40-inch class or even bigger are taken or at least hooked!

There is a social aspect to fishing Charlestown Breachway that is what New England surf fishing is all about. Friendships are renewed each season, stories and lies are swapped, anglers who are gone are remembered and there is no better place for a novice to start the life-long process of learning to fish for striped bass.

Shrimp Fly Teasers

One of the most effective teasers to use for both striped bass as well as hickory shad is a shrimp fly teaser. These can be tied very easily. Using a size 2 or 4 hook, wrap your thread to the rear. At this point, tie in body material. Olive or gray chenille or wool are effective. Wrap the body material onto the front and tie off. Now add a piece of deer hair that extends beyond the bend of the hook. Push the deer hair up to the eye of the hook and tie so that the front hairs pop up, Muddler style. Pull the hairs back with your fingers and tie off the head. Now, lay the hair along the top of the fly's body and tie it down at the bend of the hook with several ties of the thread. Finish it off with a Whip Finish. The hairs beyond the tie at the bend of the hook will form the shrimp's tail.

D. Pickering

This set up was spotted next to the breachway at Charlestown Beach.

A boater runs Charlestown Breachway on a calm day.

Lag Times in the Breachways

One of the most confusing aspects of fishing Rhode Island's breachways is dealing with the lag times. Lag times are tidal delays, the differences between what the tide is doing in the breachways as opposed to the tidal stage in the ocean (most Rhode Island tides are based on Newport tides). Those lag times are caused by the constricted breachway, or outflow waters, that lead to tidal ponds in back. At the high end of the tide, the water will not start flowing out of places like Charlestown, Quonny and Weekapaug breachways until two to three hours after the high tide is reached in the ocean. At the low end, the water will continue to flow out of the breachway for three to four hours after the low tide occurs. At the Galilee Channel expect the water to flow inward 45 minutes after the high tide is reached, and it will continue to flow outward 1 1/2 hours after the low has been reached. Factors such as tide heights, moon stage, wind and surf conditions can greatly affect the lag times.

D. Pickering

Matunuck Beach, Deep Hole,
Mantunuck

Directions:

From Route 1 in South Kingstown, follow Matunuck Beach Road south 1.3 miles, then east for 0.5 miles to the DEM fishermen's access parking lot on the right.

One of the first places that Ocean State saltwater fishermen go to shake off the cobwebs of winter is **Matunuck Beach**. This is because, for reasons that are not understood, the first schoolie stripers of the season seem to always show up here and at the West Wall, which can be seen to the east from **Deep Hole**. It may be because the rocky bottom of Carpenter's Bar off the beach or the drop-off at Deep Hole are natural striper magnets.

From the parking area, Deep Hole is a short walk to the east and is easily identified by the way the ocean waves dissipate as they wrap

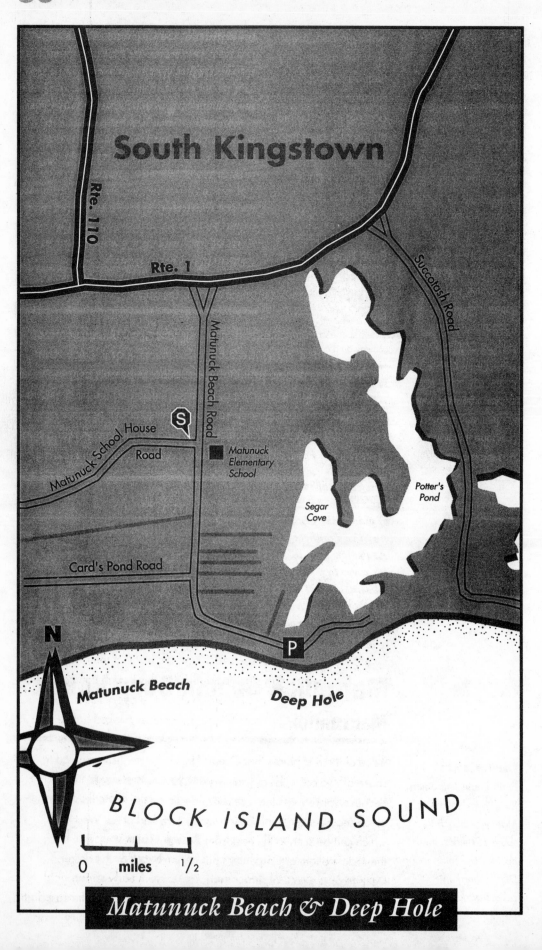

South Kingstown

Rte. 110

Rte. 1

Succotash Road

Matunuck Beach Road

Matunuck School House
Road

S

■ Matunuck
Elementary
School

Segar
Cove

Potter's
Pond

Card's Pond Road

P

N

Matunuck Beach

Deep Hole

BLOCK ISLAND SOUND

0   miles   1/2

Matunuck Beach & Deep Hole

The rocky bar at Deep Hole is exposed at low tide and the drop-off is easily reached.

around the point. The rocks here are bowling ball sized or larger and the footing can be difficult, especially if there is any surf. Be sure to wear studded waders and step carefully. Some Matunuck regulars also wear foul-weather-gear pullover jackets and cinch them tight to their waders with a wading belt. It is unfortunate that the nastier the conditions, the better the fishing is.

Wade out along the bar and cast swimming or surface plugs to the edge of the drop-off. Some fishermen also use popping plugs with their hooks removed or wooden craft-store eggs to propel leadered streamer flies, or teasers, out into the white water.

In the other direction down the beach is another prime spot, Carpenter's Bar. This is a rocky area out a good distance from the beach. The best fishing is where the white water makes up. Not a spot for the beginner, Carpenter's should be fished on the last half of the outgoing and first half of the incoming tide only, as there is an area of deeper water between the beach and the bar that must be crossed to reach the best fishing. As the tide floods, this trough can quickly become too deep to wade. It too is lined with slippery rocks from softball to bowling ball size. But the reason experienced hands take this chance is that Carpenter's is the best place to look for something bigger than a schoolie.

As the tide reaches full flood, you can still have a good chance of finding some stripers (or a little later in the season, bluefish) anywhere along the sandy beach to the west of Carpenter's.

Matunuck is a small, fisherman-friendly community that has mercifully escaped most of the glitz and over-building of other southern New England beachfront towns. From early spring right through the fall run, the fishing is very good and the ambiance is laid back and friendly.

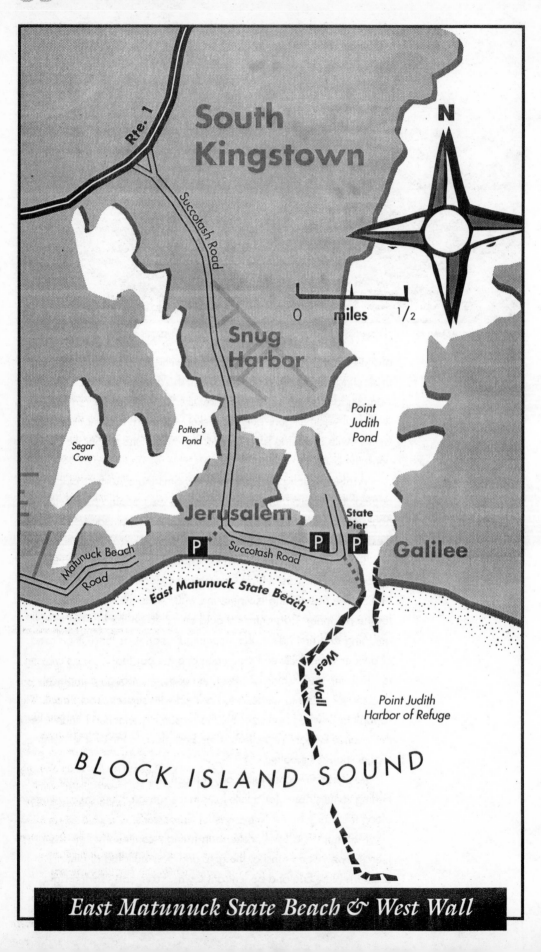

East Matunuck State Beach & West Wall

Float-and-Jig Rig

If you want to fish a bucktail jig in a rocky area or an area with a lot of obstructions, you must fish it using a float-and-jig rig. This rig, developed along the Rhode Island shore decades ago, still accounts for big catches of striped bass every spring and fall. The rig is set up with a large wooden float as the casting weight. The best homemade float to use for casting is an egg float. Wooden eggs can be purchased in craft stores. Prepare the float for fishing by drilling and then adding through-wire construction, or use screw eyes at each end. A 2- to 3-foot section of heavy monofilament is tied to the float and a small jig (under 1/2 ounce) is tied to the mono, completing the rig. The rig is simply cast out and reeled in slowly, letting waves and current impart action to the jig. Small boat fishermen can drift or slowly troll this rig.

D. Pickering

East Matunuck State Beach,
South Kingstown/Narragansett

Directions:

From Route 1 in South Kingstown, follow Succotash Road south 1.7 miles to the State Beach parking area. This is a paid parking area, open from 9 A.M. until sunset in the summer and 24 hours in the spring and fall.

Located between Matunuck Point and Deep Hole and the West Wall, this mile-long stretch of beach is often one of the most productive fishing spots on the south shore in the fall. There is some deep water close to the water's edge here (compared to other South County beaches) and when a strong southwest wind combines with a good-sized ocean swell, big bluefish and stripers can be taken very close to shore. Plugging, bottom fishing and casting live eels all work here, and if the wind isn't too strong, this is a good place to fly-fish.

The western end of the beach has a bottom of cobblestones and is a good place to look for stripers after dark. Toward the eastern end and the beginning of the West Wall, squid strips fished on the bottom often yield big fluke. Because this is a very popular swimming beach and access to the middle area is limited in the summer, most people fish the length of the beach in the spring and fall. However, it is possible to walk down from the parking areas near the West Wall and fish during the pre-dawn or evening hours during the summer; this is when you'll have the best action anyway.

Mole Crabs for Bass

One of the largest concentrations of mole crabs in the state can be found along the low surfline at East Matunuck State Beach. This is a very effective bait to use for striped bass, and it is very simple to gather your own supply. These round sand crabs burrow into the sand and can be dug at low tide. Simply dig into the sand at the water's edge with your hands. When you find something that feels like a small stone, it is probably a mole crab. Place them in a pail that has both sand and water in it. Impaled on a hook and fished on a fishfinder rig, they are an effective bait to use at night along sandy beaches.

D. Pickering

Anglers head to the West Wall for a morning of fishing.

If you look west from the beginning of the West Wall, you'll see East Matunuck State Beach.

West Wall,
Jerusalem, Narragansett

Directions:
From Route 1 in South Kingstown, follow Succotash Road south 1.7 miles, then east 0.5 mile to a small traffic island where the road turns north. Park on the left or continue 200 yards north to the parking area at the State Pier on the right.

Along with the breachways farther west and Point Judith to the east, the **West Wall** is one of the most famous and productive shore-fishing locations in Rhode Island. This is because just about every fish that swims close to shore in the Ocean State can be caught here at some point in the season, and there is plenty of room to spread out.

The Point Judith Harbor of Refuge was created with the construction of nearly three miles of stone breakwaters to protect the breachway and provide a safe refuge for ships travelling from Boston to New York. The West Wall of this refuge was soon found to be a great place to fish. The current sweeps by the east side of the Wall as the tide drops in Point Judith Salt Pond, a virtual conveyor belt of food for the waiting gamefish.

This is the most popular place in the state to seek out the first schoolie stripers each April. Whether or not this is actually the first place they show up each year is open to debate, but many Rhode Island anglers think so, and when the first striper is landed at the Wall, it marks the unofficial opening of striper season. Light tackle is popular here in the early season and many fishermen do well with small white jigs or single-hook soft plastic lures.

Bluefish and squeteague can be taken here too in the early season and again in the fall when schools of baby bunker invade the harbor. This is also a very popular location for fishermen who prefer bottom fishing for fluke, scup and black sea bass. Just remember that the bottom has many snags, so be prepared to lose some terminal tackle.

The West Wall offers plenty of room to spread out and fish.

In the fall, schools of bonito and false albacore run up and down both sides of the Wall. And although the bass and bluefishing is often better after dark, the small tunas can be caught during broad daylight.

There are a few negative aspects of fishing the West Wall. It is a well-known and popular spot and things can get a little crazy if schools of gamefish are running up and down the jetty and anglers try to give chase, leading to a confusion of flying lures and frayed tempers. The dumping tide out of the salt pond can produce so much weed in the water that lure fishing is impossible. The port of Galilee is one of the most active commercial fishing harbors in New England, ferries leave from here to Block Island and there is a large pleasure boat fleet using this waterway, so daytime fishing in the summer is often less than ideal.

In spite of these annoyances, this is the favorite spot of many Rhode Island fishermen because of the many fishing options available from April through November.

False Albacore Trick

The West Wall is Rhode Island's premier spot to catch a false albacore from shore in September. These are not easy fish to fool. While metal lures will catch some, a better alternative is to go with a float-and-fly rig. The float is a large flat-faced piece of dowel wood that is homemade using through-wire construction or screw eyes. The best fly to use is a small, blue-tailed Lefty's Deceiver fly tied on a size 1/0 hook. The fly is attached to the float with about 2 feet of heavy monofilament. The rig is cast out and popped slowly ashore, creating a disturbance on the surface of the water. False albacore are drawn to the disturbance, probably thinking there are feeding fish around. They see the fly, and bang! Hold on for some of the wildest excitement you will ever experience from shore.

D. Pickering

Jersualem State Pier, Jerusalem, Narragansett

Looking across from Galilee, one can see the Jersualem State Pier.

Directions:

From Route 1 in South Kingstown, follow Succotash Road south 1.7 miles, then east 0.5 mile to a small traffic island where the road turns north. Park on the left or continue 200 yards north to the parking area at the state pier on the right. Do not drive down or park on the small private roads in the area.

The narrow entrance (breachway) to Point Judith Salt Pond has one of the best pier fishing locations in the state. Directly across from the bustling commercial fishing docks and ferry landing at Galilee, the **Jersualem State Pier** can accommodate a dozen or so fishermen and features good action for scup, black sea bass and fluke. After dark in the summer but especially in the fall, anglers will drift live eels or chunk bait here for bluefish and stripers. Squid are often attracted to the lights of the nearby docks and drifting a freshly jigged one can be deadly, as evidenced by the bass weighing more than 40 pounds that have been landed off the pier.

Be cautious when fishing here with children or when the deck of the pier is wet. It is covered with flat sheets of plywood in various states of repair and the footing can be dangerous. Also, because the current flows very swiftly under and around the pier, bring plenty of weights if you intend to bottom fish and be prepared to lose some gear.

Pier Tactics

Piers are interesting places to fish, especially at night. Lighted piers often produce strong shadowlines very close to the pier. They also offer deep water and structure for wary fish to hide near. When fishing these places, the most productive spots will be the shadowlines. To fish close to these lines, simply drop a bucktail jig or bait straight down and walk it along the pier, jigging as you walk. It's sort of like trolling, but in this case, you are the boat. Bucktail jigs should be bounced along while you walk. Swimmers can also be cast parallel to the pier and retrieved along the shadowline. Be cautious of where you stand, since a light in back of you can cast your moving shadow into the water as you walk. That may spook wary fish.

D. Pickering

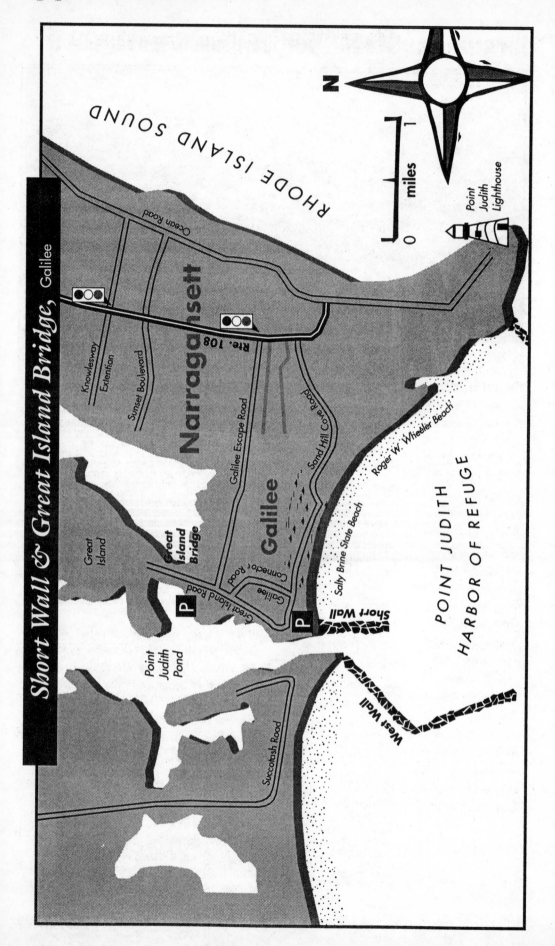

Short Wall & Great Island Bridge, Galilee

RHODE ISLAND SOUND

N

miles

1

0

Point Judith Lighthouse

Ocean Road

Narragansett

Knowlesway Extention

Sunset Boulevard

Rte. 108

Galilee Escape Road

Sand Hill Cove Road

Galilee

Great Island

Great Island Bridge

Connector Road

Great Island Road

Galilee

Point Judith Pond

Succotash Road

Short Wall

West Wall

Roger W. Wheeler Beach

Salty Brine State Beach

POINT JUDITH HARBOR OF REFUGE

Short Wall, Galilee, Narragansett

The Block Island Ferry passes the Short Wall in Galilee on its way into Block Island Sound.

Directions:

From the junction of Route 1 and Route 108 in Narragansett, follow Route 108 south (Old Point Judith Road) 3.7 miles to Galilee Escape Road on the right. Follow Galilee Escape Road west 1 mile to Great Island Road. Follow Great Island Road south 1 mile toward the entrance of Point Judith Pond and Salty Brine State Beach. Park along the street or at various pay-to-park lots. Short Wall jetty is adjacent to Salty Brine State Beach.

This is the eastern side of the narrow outlet to Point Judith Pond in Galilee, the most active commercial fishing port in Rhode Island and one of the manmade breachways of the south coast. Because of the heavy boat traffic in and out of the pond, including the Block Island Ferry, daytime bottom fishing in the channel is the best bet here in the summer. **Short Wall** is a great place to take kids to catch scup, and the constantly changing scene will keep them entertained even if the fishing is slow.

In the fall, the end of the jetty is a good place to cast to the schools of bluefish and false albacore that invade the Harbor of Refuge. Live eels drifted out on the dropping tide account for some big stripers, too. This method is most effective late at night when the boat traffic is minimal.

Swimmers in the Strike Zone

Walled breachways like the Galilee Channel offer great fishing for large stripers, especially on a dropping tide at night. Swimmers or large bucktail jigs are the best artificials to use in flows like these. The key to success in these spots is to keep your lure in the strike zone. That zone is close to the jetty rocks where the water drops off, or it is about 20 feet out from the jetty rocks.

Most experienced jetty fishermen will make short casts nearly parallel to the jetty and let the current swing the lure in close to the rocks. Once close to the rocks, begin the retrieve. Inexperienced jetty fishermen make the mistake of making long casts to non-productive waters. Shore fishermen who fish places like the Galilee channel often prefer the low end of the outgoing tide.

D. Pickering

This boy fishes the Short Wall with the watchful guidance of his adult mentor.

Great Island Bridge,
Galilee, Narragansett

The Great Island Bridge affords a view of Potter's Pond.

Directions:

From the junction of Route 1 and Route 108 in Narragansett, follow Route 108 south (Old Point Judith Road) 3.7 miles to Galilee Escape Road on the right. Follow Galilee Escape Road west 1 mile to Great Island Road. Park next to the bridge in the municipal lot.

Easy access and good fishing for a variety of species make **Great Island Bridge** attractive to novices and experienced fishermen alike. Youngsters and physically challenged anglers can fish from the bulkhead next to the bridge on the southwest side for scup, flounder and tautog. The swift flow under the bridge attracts stripers and squeteague, especially in the early season and after dark right into the fall.

Inside the bridge to the east, the marsh edges are a great place to fly-fish for stripers after dark.

Shadowlines

Shadowlines are formed at night where lights, such as streetlights on a bridge, cast their glow on the water. They are well defined where the streetlights intersect the dark shadow under the bridge. Shadowlines are prime places to fish because baitfish are often drawn to the lighted side of the line, while large predators, such as striped bass, blues and hickory shad, lurk on the dark side of the line.

The smart fisherman tries to fish his artificial, such as a bucktail jig or swimmer, right along the shadowline. Better still, the offering may be cast into the lighted area and drifted into the dark side of the line where most of the hits will occur. Fishermen who work these shadowlines often cast from atop a bridge or down below from the sides if possible.

D. Pickering

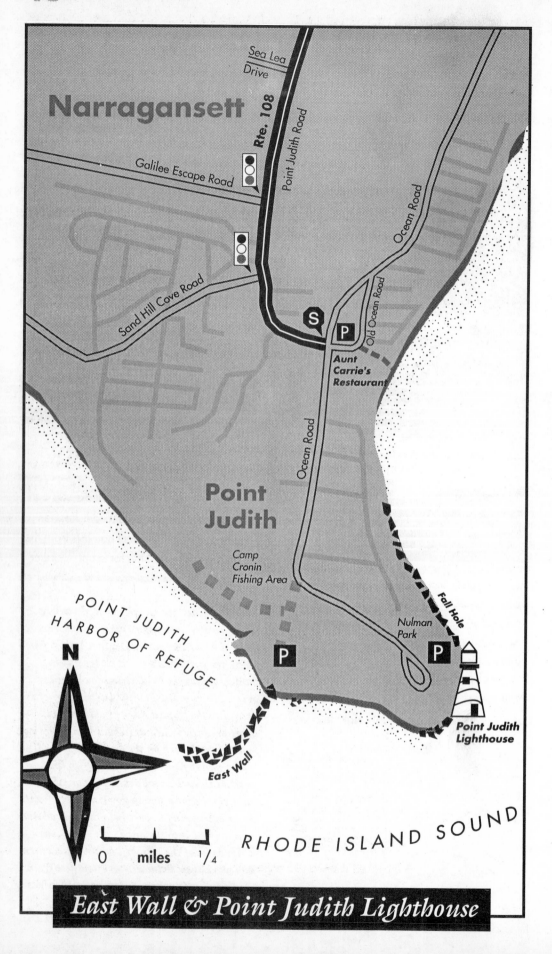

Narragansett

Sea Lea Drive

Rte. 108

Point Judith Road

Galilee Escape Road

Ocean Road

Sand Hill Cove Road

Old Ocean Road

S

P

Aunt Carrie's Restaurant

Ocean Road

Point Judith

Camp Cronin Fishing Area

Nulman Park

Fall Hole

POINT JUDITH

HARBOR OF REFUGE

N

P

P

East Wall

Point Judith Lighthouse

RHODE ISLAND SOUND

0 miles ¹/₄

East Wall & Point Judith Lighthouse

High surf and good fishing are often found at the East Wall.

East Wall,
Point Judith, Narragansett

Directions:

From the junction of Route 1 and Route 108 in Narragansett, follow Route 108 south 4 miles to Ocean Road. Follow Ocean Road south 0.6 mile to the Camp Cronin Fishing Area access road and the parking lot on the right.

There are three seasons for fishing the **East Wall**: early season for stripers and the first bluefish; mid season daytime fishing for scup, fluke and black sea bass; and, the most popular, the fall run of big stripers, bluefish and false albacore.

The East Wall protects the Harbor of Refuge in Point Judith/Galilee and is a very popular spot, not only because the fishing is generally very good, but also because there is plenty of parking and anglers can also fish the shore toward

The remains of a World War II gun mount are still visible at the East Wall.

Point Judith itself. The rocky shore toward the lighthouse often has great striper fishing, especially when there is a southwest breeze pushing bait into the shore. Although this shoreline can become choked with weeds, especially if a large swell is running or it has been stormy, many anglers like to cast surface plugs here or fish live eels after dark. The area just to the left of the parking lot in front of

Bait fisherman cast off the East Wall.

the remains of a large gun mount (part of the coastal defenses in World War II) is a popular spot.

In the summer the East Wall is a very popular spot for families to fish for scup and fluke. Caution should be exercised here when fishing with small children, however, as large swells sometimes sweep down the length of the wall. It is difficult to approach the water from the jetty regardless of the ocean conditions. Stout gear is the rule, so that fish can be lifted over the rocks. Some anglers prefer to fish along the protected beach inside the wall, away from the swells, and casting live eels here after dark in the summer can yield big striped bass.

The fall striper run is when the East Wall really comes into its own. Local fishing clubs plan yearly outings to the East Wall for the great autumn action, and it is only a short drive from the camping area at Fishermen's Memorial State Park. Big bluefish are often taken here too and schools of false albacore charge around the Harbor of Refuge, often within a cast of the East Wall.

What's Up With Scup?
Scup, often called the sunfish of the sea, can be caught off the East Wall in big numbers. Bottom bait fishermen line the jetty like a picket fence, casting their offer-ings of squid or pieces of seaworms to schools of scup that inhabit these waters. The bite is a summer one, with the months of June, July and August being productive. Fishing is best in the daytime. There's nothing sophisticated about the rigs used, just a sinker on the terminal end and a couple of hooks knotted up above. Use small pieces of bait and prepare for nonstop action at times. Those who put in their time may be rewarded with limits of good table fare.

D. Pickering

The sandy beach next to the East Wall can also be productive.

This angler fishes the East Wall, with the Point Judith Lighthouse visible in the distance.

Surf sweeps around Point Judith.

Point Judith Lighthouse,
Narragansett

Directions:

From the junction of Route 1 and Route 108 in Narragansett, follow Route 108 south 4 miles to Ocean Road. Go south on Ocean Road 0.8 mile to the parking area at the lighthouse (Nulman Park).

There have probably been more big stripers taken from the rocks around **Point Judith** than anywhere else in the Ocean State, but great care should be taken. When a big swell is running, this is a place for experienced surf fishermen only, as the rocks are covered with a black slime that is treacherous. Even when the waves are small, footing is tricky, so Korkers or studded-soled waders are a must and a self-inflating personal floatation devise is a good idea, too. Experienced surfhands always take a few minutes to observe the surf before wading in to get an idea of the frequency and size of the sets of waves.

This area should really be thought of as three locations, all within an easy walk of the parking area: the east side below the old restaurant and Nulman Park, known locally as the Fall Hole; the bars off the point itself; and the deep hole to the west of the point. Although fish can be taken at all these

Directly in front of the lighthouse the footing is trecherous, as it is throughout most of the area.

locations all season with nighttime being best in the summer, Point Jude really comes into its own in the fall during the southward migration of stripers and bluefish. If a northeast storm is brewing, so much the better. Crashing waves, wheeling birds and the foghorn sounding as big swimming plugs are cast into the foam are what fishing the Light is all about.

An angler fishes in the rocks below Nulman Park.

When a swell from the south sweeps around the point, the east side rocks below Nulman Park can be very productive. Try pencil poppers or surface swimmers cast in the troughs between the waves, or swimmers, jigs or live eels right in the wash. You'll lose a few plugs to the many large and small boulders that are just below the surface, but there are often big stripers here. The first few hours of an easterly wind as a storm approaches are considered prime time here. This spot is called the Fall Hole by some, a clue to what time of the year it fishes the best.

Walk through the grounds of the lighthouse and just to the left of the point and you'll see a small set of stairs through the seawall leading down to the rocks. There is a rocky bar off the point where stripers and bluefish search for any bait that gets swept into the turbulence. Surface plugs are your best bet here. This is another spot that can be very dangerous in high surf, so exercise extreme caution when approaching the water's edge. If possible, fish here the first time with someone who knows where safe footing can be found or observe where and how the veterans work the surf.

To the right of the point as you face the water, the shoreline curves to the northwest. Inside this small cove is a deep hole and some large boulders along the shore. The advantage of fishing here is that you don't need to be a competition-rated caster; the fish come in quite close and this is an ideal place to cast and retrieve live eels after dark. The disadvantage is that the water gets quite churned up on this south-facing shore after a large swell or a hard southwest blow and the water can be too weedy to fish.

Between these three areas, you should always be able to find a place to fish in all but the worst conditions. Point Judith is a productive and challenging fishing spot that yields more trophy-sized stripers and bluefish every year than anywhere else in the state.

To the right of Point Judith Lighthouse you can see the East Wall.

A Fifty On A Popper

   Mix the rocky bars along Point Judith with intermittent boulders that line the bottom and throw in a little white water and you've got the perfect recipe for a big-bass hangout. The problem for surf fishermen at Point Judith is being able to make a long cast to reach the most productive water. About the best plug to beat these conditions is a popper. Here the popper rules and has been blasted in recent years by enormous bass up to 50 pounds in broad daylight. The best color is white or a blue-headed/white-bodied model. These colors simulate squid, which have been known to come close to shore along here. The best conditions under which to fish a popper in this spot are stiff onshore winds in your teeth with a charged-up surf.

                                                              D. Pickering

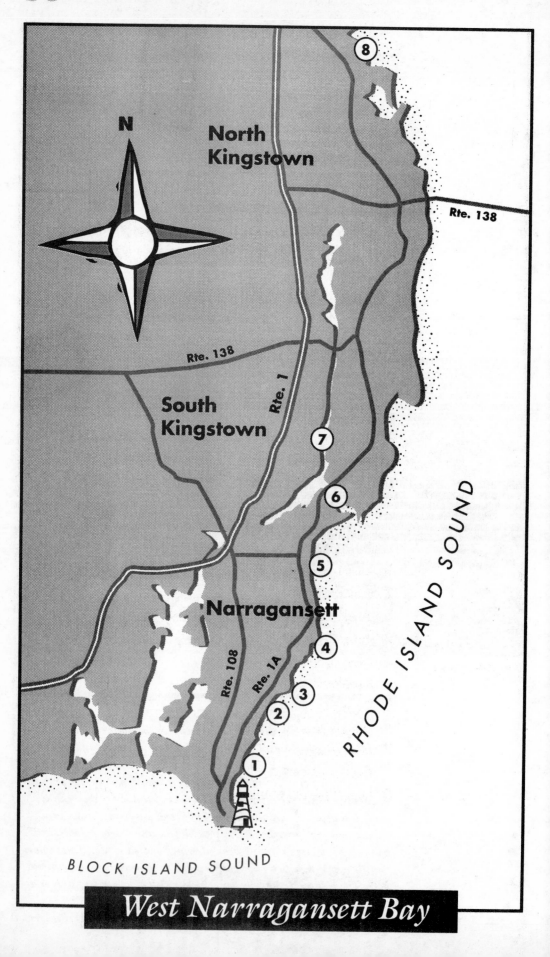

N

North
Kingstown

Rte. 138

Rte. 138

Rte. 1

South
Kingstown

⑦

⑥

⑤

Narragansett

RHODE ISLAND SOUND

Rte. 108

Rte. 1A

④

③

②

①

BLOCK ISLAND SOUND

West Narragansett Bay

West Narragansett Bay

The southwestern shore of Narragansett Bay, from the Narrow River in the town of Narragansett to Point Judith, is a surfcaster's paradise. Strong currents and ocean swells sweep this six-mile stretch of shoreline, and there are dozens of prime fishing spots, ranging from sandy beaches to rocky points. Striped bass, bluefish, fluke, blackfish, squeteague and scup can be caught here. In the fall, this is one of the best areas for the shore-bound fisherman to try for bonito and false albacore. Just around Point Judith to the south are more good locations for almost a half-mile of shoreline to the East Wall. In fact, there are so many choices along this relatively small section of coastline that many fishermen won't fish anywhere else.

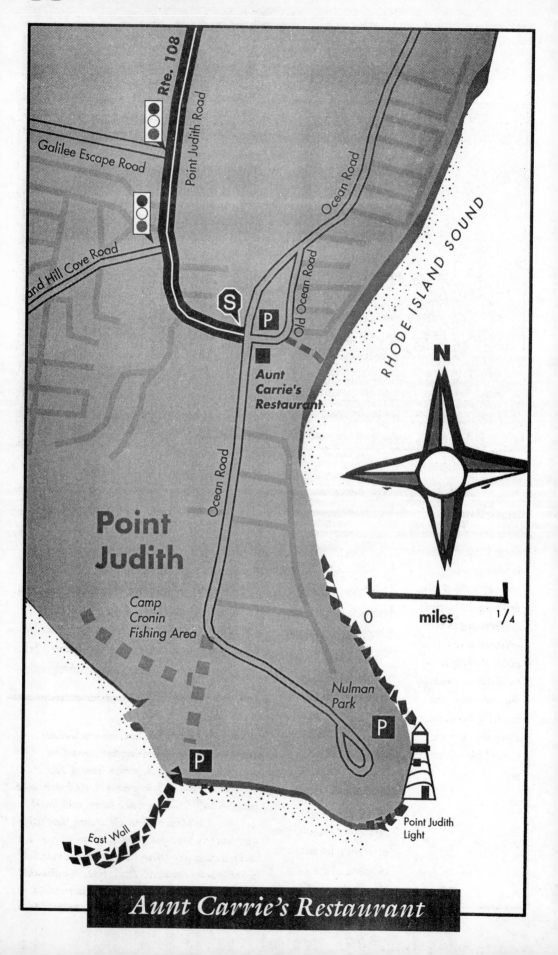

Rte. 108

Point Judith Road

Galilee Escape Road

Ocean Road

and Hill Cove Road

Old Ocean Road

S

P

Aunt Carrie's Restaurant

Ocean Road

Point Judith

Camp Cronin Fishing Area

RHODE ISLAND SOUND

N

0   **miles**   1/4

Nulman Park

P

P

East Wall

Point Judith Light

Aunt Carrie's Restaurant

Aunt Carrie's Restaurant,
Narragansett

In front of Aunt Carrie's restaurant looking north, the angler faces a rocky, open-ocean shoreline.

Directions:

From the intersection of Route 1 and Route 108 in Narragansett, proceed south 4 miles on Route 108 (Point Judith Road) to the intersection of Ocean Road. Parking is available across from the restaurant, and access to the shore is down the dirt road behind the restaurant.

Only a little more than a half-mile from the Point Judith light, the east-facing shoreline of bowling-ball-sized rocks and scattered boulders in front of **Aunt Carrie's Restaurant**, is a good place to cast plugs or live eels after dark in the summer or by day in the spring and especially the fall. Primarily a striper and bluefish spot, sometimes false albacore work along this shore in the fall, giving shore-bound anglers a shot at these speedy fish. If there has been an extended period of east wind, this spot can weed up too much to fish. What makes this location attractive is the easy access, relatively safe fishing conditions (except during very stormy conditions), plenty of parking nearby, the possibility of finding some very large stripers and bluefish, and the proximity (in season) of some of the best clam cakes in Rhode Island!

A Secret Spot?

Behind the famed clamcakes-n-chowda restaurant lies a parking lot covered in stones, beyond that the green-blue of the Atlantic. To the right and left, the beach looks remarkably similar, stone shore, with boulders here, boulders there. Of course, that is just our human's eye perspective. If we were a striped bass, our thoughts would no doubt be more results oriented. More like, "Crabs and lobsters ready to eat under here; silversides tumbling in the wash over there; rocks to hide

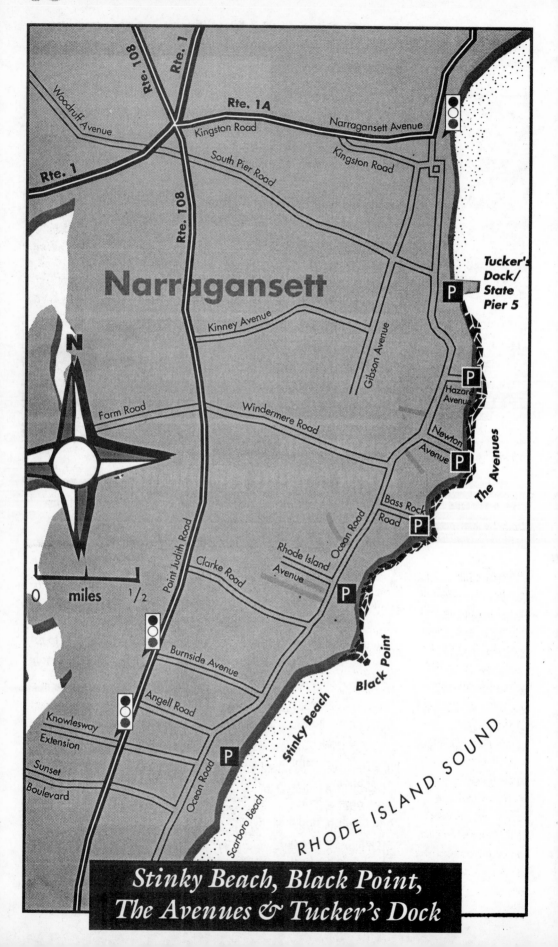

Rte. 108

Rte. 1

Rte. 1A

Woodruff Avenue

Kingston Road

Narragansett Avenue

South Pier Road

Kingston Road

Rte. 1

Rte. 108

Narragansett

Kinney Avenue

Gibson Avenue

N

Farm Road

Windermere Road

Hazard Avenue

Newton Avenue

The Avenues

Bass Rock Road

Ocean Road

Rhode Island Avenue

Point Judith Road

Clarke Road

0 miles 1/2

Burnside Avenue

Black Point

Angell Road

Knowlesway Extension

Stinky Beach

Sunset Boulevard

Ocean Road

Scarboro Beach

Tucker's Dock/ State Pier 5

RHODE ISLAND SOUND

Stinky Beach, Black Point, The Avenues & Tucker's Dock

behind; I like it here a lot!" Yet for all its structure and possibilities, Aunt Carries gets little pressure. Or does it...

This location lies in Narragansett, where the surfcasters live and die never revealing the whole truth. In a sport known for its secretive nature, Narragansett's fishermen are among the most guarded. Even older fishermen who no longer fish need to be bribed with imported ale before the screws at the back of their tongues become loosened. The locals are known to be so secretive that, several years ago two Narragansett surfcasters were chosen to fill the envelopes with the results of the Academy Award nominations.

Long ago, there was a pair of commercial rod-and-reel fishermen who would launch a rowboat along this shore and troll a live eel off the stern. Back and forth, close to the shore they would row, filling their boat with bass. They were known to have cleaned up on regular occasions. I would assume a kayak would work in a similar fashion, but as far as I know, no one has attempted it.

Now, this area is known simply as Behind Aunt Carrie's and tends to attract mainly older surfcasters, known as sharpies. It gets some pressure in the fall from retirees from who like to baitfish. Most of the chunkers set up directly in front of the parking area and sit in lawn chairs waiting for a bite. There is a reason they don't venture too far. These bony beaches are notoriously hard to walk; you have to pick your way along slowly, planting your foot deliberately, so as not to turn an ankle.

This combination of mystery and tough footing mark Aunt Carrie's as one of the least-pressured spots in Narragansett. Or is it...

J. Lyons

Stinky Beach, Narragansett

Directions:

From the intersection of Route 1 and Route 108 in Narragansett, follow Route 108 (Point Judith Road) south 2.9 miles to Angell Road on the left. Follow Angell Road 0.5 mile to the intersection of Ocean Road. Parking at Scarborough State Beach lots on Ocean Road is available until 11 P.M. in the summer and on the access road into the park in the off season.

This colorfully named spot is actually the north end of Scarborough State Beach and is most easily accessed from that area, although this involves a bit of a hike. That may not be a bad thing, though, because in the fall bluefish and bass often push bait (in recent years, peanut bunker) right onto the sandy beach, and it's worth casting as you walk north toward Black Point. **Stinky Beach** is the last section before the beach ends and the rocky shores begin again. It is a place where the southwest wind and predatory gamefish trap bait, and the fishing can be spectacular. This is also a good place to swim a live eel after dark. That same southwest wind can also stack up a huge amount of seaweed here, though, which is what gives the beach its name. Don't neglect the area where the rocks start, either, and if you're ambitious, you can continue along the shore and fish your way all the to Black Point.

All The Weed You Want

Stinky Beach only really stinks after a strong east wind has blown for a couple of days. The seaweed has a tendency to pile up here, on the north end of Scarborough Beach. A strong easterly flow pushes the weed up high on the beach and there it stays. After a few day of baking it begins to rot and stink, hence the name.

Back in Colonial times farmers would use seaweed for fertilizer. The farmers would haul the weed off the beach in oxcarts. The gathering of seaweed was so important that many of the right-of-ways that we now enjoy for surfcasting were created so inland farmers could be assured of ocean access to acquire the seaweed. The Rhode Island Constitution ensures shore access for all residents, holding the shoreline below mean high water in the public domain for a variety of activities, mentioning the collection of seaweed as one.

Many years ago at Narragansett Town Beach a man protesting the beach access fee showed up at the gate with a wheel barrel and pitchfork as well as a fishing pole and some other gear. He stated he was there to exercise his privileges as a Rhode Island resident. He refused to pay the beach fee, citing the Rhode Island Constitution and was subsequently arrested. The man's action was a case of civil disobedience. The man reasoned that charging him a fee to walk through the right-of-way was a violation of his constitutional rights.

He lost and Narragansett Town Beach still charges by the head to enter during beach hours. But there is no fee to walk onto Stinky Beach, and you can fill your oxcart with all the seaweed you want.

J. Lyons

Black Point, Narragansett

Directions:

From the intersection of Route 1 and Route 108 in Narragansett, follow Route 108 (Point Judith Road) south 2.9 miles to Angell Road on the left. Follow Angell Road 0.5 mile to the intersection of Ocean Road. Follow Ocean Road north for 1 mile to the DEM Fisherman's Access parking area on the right.

Black Point is the beginning of the area known to locals as the High Rocks, stretching from here, north along this western shore of the Bay for about two miles to the beach at Narragansett Pier. This is very productive striper water, and in the fall false albacore can sometimes be taken here. A light to moderate southwest wind can make casting difficult, but some local fly-fishermen work around the rocks here because the fish will often be close in and long casts aren't mandatory. Be sure to wear Korkers or similar footgear, and avoid stepping on any ledges or rocks that are covered with black slime or seaweed.

In the fall Black Point is one of the more popular destinations in the Narragansett area, so expect some company if the word is out that the stripers are around.

Nighttime Eeling Tips

About the easiest and most effective route to a big bass is by slinging live eels at night. Here are some tricks that may lead to success and may also make eel fishing easier. Keep your eels on ice. It will make handling them much easier. Before hooking, give the eel's head a few bangs on a rock or the side of a bucket to stun it. This will prevent or at least discourage the eel from balling up on the hook.

Make your eel-fishing rigs ahead of time. These rigs are made with 2 to 3 feet of heavy

From Stinky Beach you can see Black Point to the north.

mono and have a hook snelled to one end and a swivel tied to the other. Make at least half a dozen and store them in leader wallets. Use circle hooks for catch-and-release fishing.

Move around from rock pile to rock pile, since mobility is the key to success in eel fishing. Cast the eel out and retrieve slowly, keeping the rod tip high. Allow a fish to pull the rod down to the water and then pull back hard. Finally, scout the area in the daytime for prime casting locations.

D. Pickering

Hazard Avenue, Newton Aveue
Bass Rock Road, Narragansett

Directions:

From the intersection of Route 1, Route 108 and Route 1A in Narragansett, travel east on Route 1A (Kingstown Road into Narragansett Avenue) 1.3 miles to Narragansett Town Beach and the intersection of Ocean Road. Follow Ocean Road south along the water to Hazard Avenue on the left (1.2 miles), Newton Avenue

There can be great fishing at these spots, but there is also significant danger. In fact, many Rhody fishermen feel these are the most dangerous locations to shore fish in the state. The granite shelves and outcroppings slope toward the crashing surf, and many fatalities have occurred here over the years. Stout surfcasting equipment is the rule, so that hooked fish may be dragged out of the waves and up the rocks without having to approach the edge of the water. Korkers and a self-inflating life vest are required equipment, too, and if you do have the misfortune to slip, remember to swim out and away from the rocks, rather than trying to climb back up. This is because most of these ledges cover deep undercuts that victims may be forced down into by the pounding swells as they try to climb back up the slippery rock faces. This is no place to fish with small children or anyone who does not know how to read the water. And the worst part is that this area fishes best when the wind is from the northeast and the weather is the worst.

This spincaster works the white water off Hazard Avenue.

From the rocks off Newton Avenue an angler can look toward Narragansett Bay.

on the left (1.6 miles) and Bass Rock Road on the left (2 miles). There is limited parking available at the end of each road.

In spite of the danger, many Rhode Island surfcasters count these spots among their favorites because trophy-sized stripers cruise the edges of the cliffs and drop-offs. Try large swimming plugs or metal lures. Some anglers also bring along specially made long-handled gaffs to drag fish up the rocks.

Just remember, **Hazard Avenue** came by its name for very good reason; the other spots are just as dangerous. This coastline is a wild and beautiful place from which you can marvel at the ocean's power, but be sure to exercise great care and never turn your back on the waves!

Hazard Avenue can be a dangerous spot to fish, but it offers a good chance at trophy stripers.

White Water, The Surfcaster's Edge

White water is a surf-fishing condition that can suddenly light up the fishing. The action of strong waves pushed ashore by onshore breezes sets up a ribbon of foamy and turbulent white water along a rocky shoreline. In this area of Narragansett a moderate northeast wind can set up some very productive white water. It is within the turbulence of the white water that stripers love to lurk to ambush prey. Smart shore fishermen should focus their attention in close by working their artificials in the white water. Lures that work below the surface, such as bucktail jigs (on a float or along the bottom) or straight-back swimmers, are especially effective in rocky areas with white water. Hits will come almost on shore. Avoid long and non-productive casts in these places.

D. Pickering

Tucker's Dock (State Pier 5),
Narragansett

Protected from swells, State Pier 5 is a great bottom-fishing location.

Directions:
From the intersection of Route 1, Route 108 and Route 1A in Narragansett, drive east on Route 1A (Kingstown Road into Narragansett Avenue) 1.3 miles to Narragansett Town Beach and the intersection of Ocean Road. Follow Ocean Road south 0.7 mile to the stone pier and parking area on the left.

This is the northern terminus of the High Rocks shoreline between Scarborough Beach and Narragansett Town Beach. With easy access, **Tucker's Dock** is a great place to take youngsters to bottom fish for scup and tautog. False albacore and bluefish often chase bait along the jetty in the fall. Although ocean swells sometimes break off the south side (local surfers love this spot!), there is a dock on the north side built against the high stone breakwater that is ideal for bait fishing.

Easy Fishing, Tough Fishing
State Pier 5 is a really easy place to fish. You are fishing from a flat surface that is lighted at night. It has something of a reputation as an amateur's spot, but it can be surprising. The fall is the best time here, particularly during the Narragansett mullet run. The bait gets stacked into the corner between the dock and the beginning of the seawall and for a while it is easy pickings.

The rocks to the north, below the seawall and up Ocean Road to the Coast Guard House are another matter. There is no way, unless you bring a ladder, to get to them, other than walking their length below the seawall, roughly a half-mile. There are perhaps only a handful of active surfmen that really know this area. It is fitting that one of Narragansett's least-known spots is in plain view, on Ocean Road. The late Narragansett tackle shop owner, guide, author and legend, Jerry Sylvester, would fish these rocks often with clients and he was a master of them.

I have Mr. Sylvester's 1956 book Salt Water Fishing Is Easy *and it is quite informative. I do not know if the author was in keeping with Narragansett's tradition of top-secret surfcasting or whether he was the one who created the culture, but you will not find much mention of specific areas inside his now out-of-print treatise. Even when describing spots for scup, the author remains guarded. The book is colored with accounts like, "trolling with an attorney from New York in a large cove," or, "I was fishing with David Niven, the movie star. We were on a rocky shore." If you know any Narragansett surfcasters and you're fortunate enough to find a copy of this book, you will soon find yourself smiling.*

J. Lyons

Narrow River/Sprague Bridge,
Narragansett

Bait fishing along the shore near Sprague Bridge is productive.

Directions:

From Route 1A (also known as Beach Street) in downtown Narragansett, follow Route 1A north for 0.5 mile to the town parking/bath house area (spring and fall only) to fish the mouth

Narrow River is the 3/4-mile outlet to a much larger estuary, the Pettaquamscutt River. At the extreme northern end of this river, near the Gilbert Stuart Homestead and Museum, is a herring run, one of the most prolific in the state (be sure to check state and local regulations before taking herring). Because of this, the Narrow River section is a very popular and productive location to fish for striped bass in the early season. Live-lined herring are best of course, but chunks of fresh dead herring drifted out at the mouth of the river during a dropping tide is another way to catch big stripers. In years past, fishermen would often take big weakfish here too, and now that

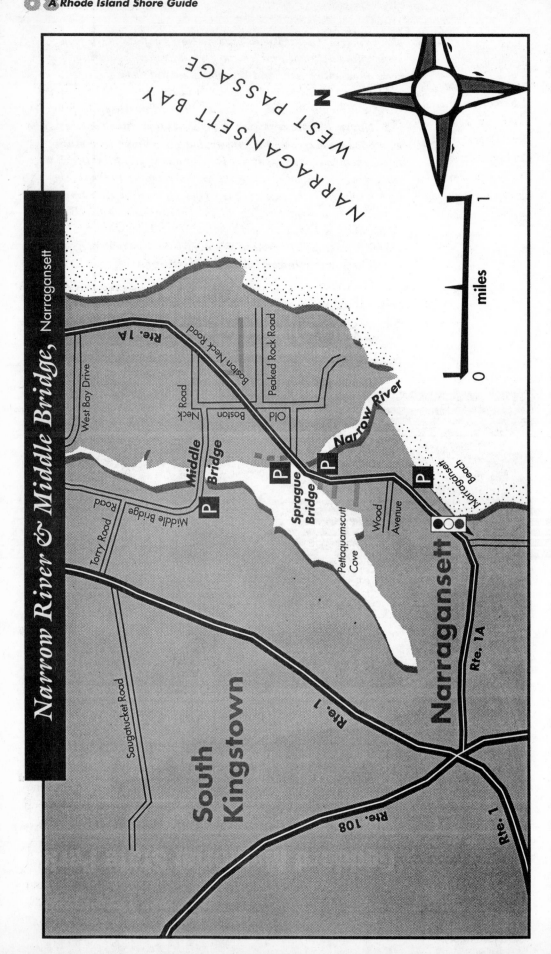

Narrow River & Middle Bridge, Narragansett

NARRAGANSETT BAY — WEST PASSAGE

N

0 1 miles

Rte. 1A

West Bay Drive

Neck Road

Boston Neck Road

Peaked Rock Road

Old Boston Neck

Narrow River

Narragansett Beach

Middle Bridge

Sprague Bridge

Middle Bridge Road

Torry Road

Wood Avenue

Pettaquamscutt Cove

Saugatucket Road

South Kingstown

Narragansett

Rte. 1A

Rte. 1

Rte. 108

Rte. 1

of the river (north from the parking lot). Or follow Route 1A north 1.5 miles from downtown Narragansett to the parking area next to the Sprague Bridge to fish the river out to the mouth.

this species is starting to reestablish itself in the Bay, this may be a good place to look for them. After dark or at first light are best.

As the season progresses, schoolie stripers invade the river and fishing from the marsh edges can be very good with light tackle and fly gear. Be careful of the drainage ditches, however, as many of them are quite steep and have a bottom of deep mud. As you work your way out toward the mouth, the channel narrows and sweeps around a point behind the private Dunes Beach Club. This is a great place to fly-fish or swim a live eel after dark. Be sure not to trespass on beach club property. In the summer the beachfront at the point and the mouth of the river are best fished in the dead of night.

This estuary system is a huge bait factory, and stripers, hickory shad and small bluefish can be found anywhere, particularly in the fall. The deep holes near the bridge are also worth a shot for flounder in the early spring and late fall. A few diehard striper fans fish the upper reaches for holdover schoolie stripers all winter long, one of the few places in Rhode Island that has winter striper fishing.

Teaser Rigs for Finicky Bass

Striped bass that feed on small sand eels and grass shrimp can be very fussy and selective if you're trying to fish an artificial. Often, a teaser is just the ticket to catching fish. Here is how to set up a teaser rig. Use two sections (18 to 20 inches) of heavy monofilament (25- to 40-pound-test). Knot these sections together with a swivel at one end, a swivel in the middle and a snap at the other end. On the front eye of each swivel, knot on a piece of mono that measures 8 to 10 inches. The teasers are attached to these short pieces of mono. Popular saltwater flies, such as Deceivers, Clousers and shrimp flies, make excellent teasers, as do commercial Red Gill teasers. Once your teaser rigs are made, place them in leader wallets for tangle-free storage.

D. Pickering

Middle Bridge/ Pettaquamscutt River, Narragansett/South Kingstown

Directions:
From downtown Narragansett, follow Route 1A north 1.8 miles to Old Boston Neck Road on the left (0.3 mile past the Sprague Bridge).

If you're a fly-fisherman or light-tackle fan, **Middle Bridge** and the **Pettaquamscutt River** estuary system are worth exploring. Follow the trails into the Narrow River Land Trust's Garrison House Acres area on the west side of the river to the marsh edges where stripers feed on abundant silversides, mummichogs and, later in the summer, baby menhaden. It is possible as the tide drops to wade to the edge of the channel and fish your way down toward

Middle Bridge offers a great view of Pettaquamscut Cove.

Follow Old Boston Neck Road north 0.3 mile to Middle Bridge Road. Follow Middle Bridge Road west for 0.6 mile. There is parking on the west side of the bridge for three cars on the south side of the street near the bridge.

Pettaquamscutt Cove and the beginning of the outflow (Narrow River). There are some deeper holes as you approach the turn into Narrow River, so be careful.

Anglers are allowed to drop a line from Middle Bridge itself and the flounder fishing can be good in the early spring and fall. Some very nice hickory shad can be taken here also.

State-Record Hickory Shad

My 3 1/2-year-old son Matt set the state record for hickory shad on November 5, 1989, when he caught a fish of 20 inches that weighed 2 pounds, 11 ounces under the Sprague Bridge at Narrow River. He used a light-spinning outfit suited for freshwater bluegills. His lure was a homemade 1/8-ounce white bucktail jig with a small plastic curly tail attached. This spot and its backwaters remain a hotspot for hickory shad to this day. Fly-fishermen and light-tackle enthusiasts flock to this spot every fall to fish for these abundant and hard-fighting gamesters.

D. Pickering

After passing the Sprague Bridge, Peggaquamscutt Cove offers a wealth of opportunities to the angler.

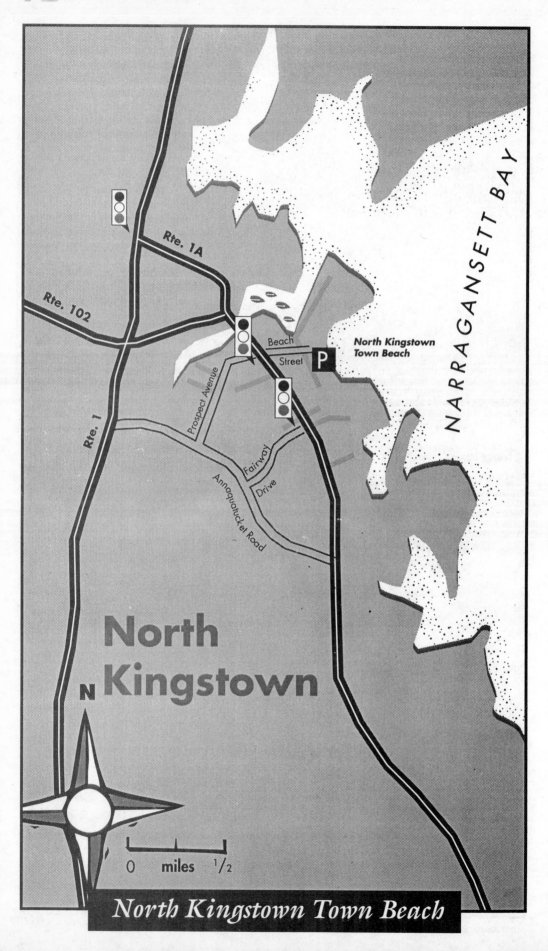

North Kingstown Town Beach

North Kingstown Town Beach,
North Kingstown

Bluefish push bait up to North Kingstown Town Beach every autumn.

Directions:

From Route 1A in North Kingstown, go east 0.25 mile to the town beach parking area.

North Kingstown Town Beach is best fished in the late summer and fall when bluefish are searching the harbors and beachfronts of interior Narragansett Bay for menhaden. A pretty town park and beach that is heavily used in the summer, this is not a place to find solitude, but it is well suited for fishing with children. Tautog and winter flounder can be caught here in the spring right off the beach. After dark in the summer and fall, fly-fishermen will walk south along the beach, around the point and fish the entrance to Duck Cove. This is especially effective when schools of baby bunker are in the area.

Peanut Bunker Tactics

Peanut bunker, or baby menhaden, invade the waters of Narragansett Bay in late summer and early fall. They attract lots of stripers and bluefish, yet when these fish start feeding on this bait, they can get mighty fussy. Here are some ways to fool fussy predators. Four-inch shad bodies in white or chartreuse and threaded onto various-sized barbed jigheads are very effective. Fish them deep under the schools of bait.

Metal lures, such as Kastmasters or Hooligans, are great to cast a long distance. Let these lures sink under the schools of bait, too. When these lures fail, go with the real thing. After snagging the baitfish with a weighted or unweighted treble hook, immediately drop the snagged bait below the school. This sure-fire method is the most effective way to fool finicky predators that lurk below the schools of peanut bunker.

D. Pickering

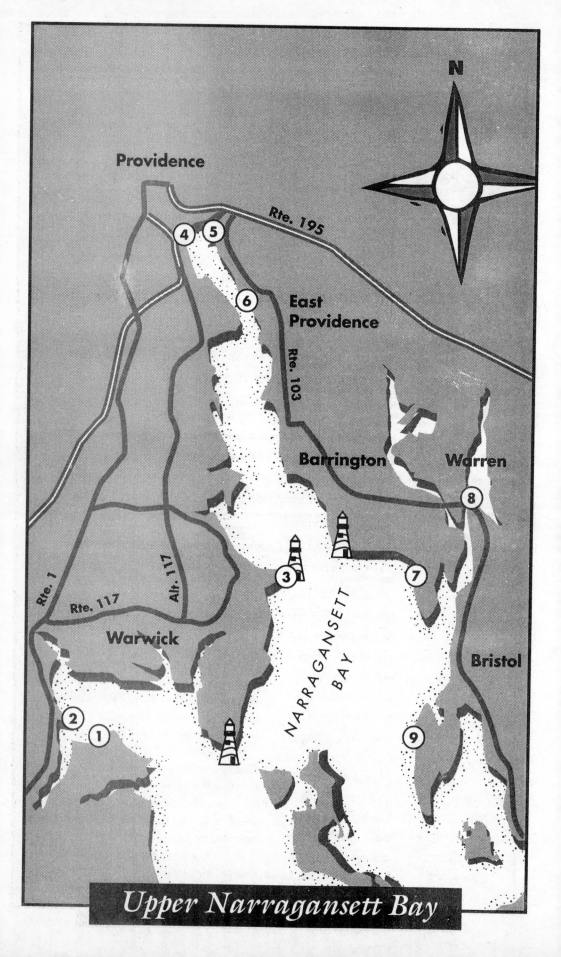

Upper Narragansett Bay

Upper Narragansett Bay

Being closer to the urban center of Providence, **upper Narragansett Bay** is more developed, and chances are you won't have a solitary fishing experience, but this shouldn't stop you from taking advantage of the angling opportunities in this area. Colt State Park in Bristol has been called the most beautiful park in the state and is only a short drive from the city. The East Providence Bike Path area may be something less than a wilderness fishing experience, but the chances are good for landing some bragging-sized fish at certain times of the year here. There is even a popular wintertime fishery for holdover schoolie stripers right in downtown Providence in the Providence River.

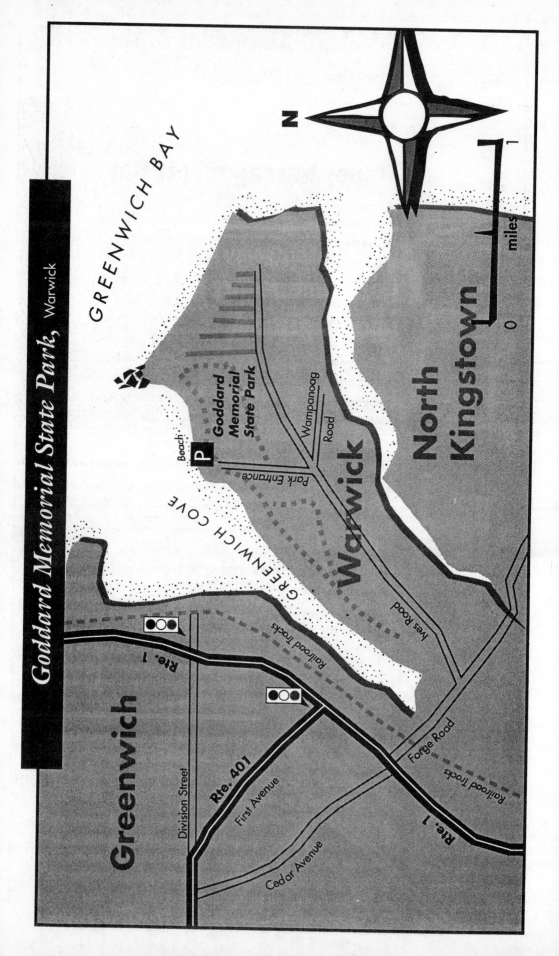

Goddard Memorial State Park, Warwick

GREENWICH BAY

N

miles

1

0

Goddard Memorial State Park

Beach

P

Park Entrance

Wampanoag Road

GREENWICH COVE

Warwick

North Kingstown

Ives Road

Railroad Tracks

Rte. 1

Greenwich

Division Street

Rte. 401

First Avenue

Cedar Avenue

Forge Road

Railroad Tracks

Rte. 1

Goddard Memorial State Park,
Warwick

Fishing is a possibile to the right of the swimming beach at Goddard Memorial State Park.

Directions:

From Route 1 in Warwick, follow Forge Road southeast 0.7 mile to Ives Road. Follow Ives Road northeast 1.6 miles to the main park entrance on the left. Follow the park road straight (northwest) 0.6 mile to the beach parking area. Goddard Park is open from sunrise to sunset.

The most popular metropolitan state recreation area in Rhode Island, **Goddard Park** was once an estate of a wealthy family. The state took possession of the 489 acres in 1927 and the park opened in 1930. Although heavily used, it remains beautiful, with rolling lawns, riding trails, a nine-hole golf course, picnic areas and a beach that fishes very well in the spring. This beach borders Greenwich Bay, which warms very quickly and is one of the first interior Narragansett Bay spots to get bluefish in late May. It is also a very good place to look for squeteague.

Because the beach is so popular, try to be there at first light, as soon as the park opens.

Fly-fishermen also do very well here for early season schoolie bass. The beach is protected from strong southwest breezes and the wading is easy.

Squeteague, Rhody Style

   Elsewhere they are called weakfish, sea trout and tiderunners, but here in Rhode Island they are called squeteague. Fishing for these fish is synonymous with light tackle. Bait fishermen like to drift worms on the bottom and often catch them along with schoolies and flounder in late spring. Those using light tackle and artificials need to think jigs.

   If you are going with bucktail jigs, use small ones weighing less than 1/2 ounce. A flathead or Upperman-style jig that is all white and tied with red thread is very effective. Be sure to thread a white plastic curly tail on the jig's hook for added action.

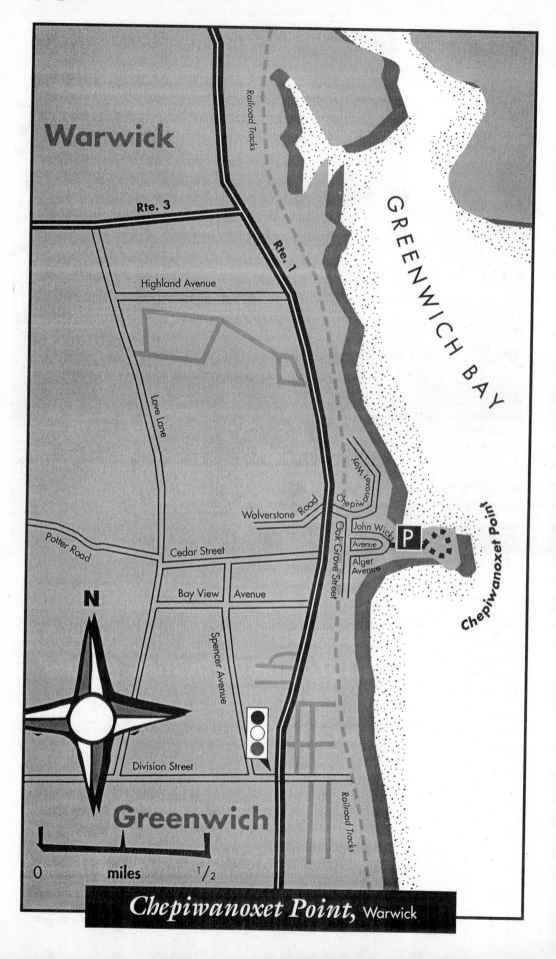

Warwick

Rte. 3

Railroad Tracks

Rte. 1

Highland Avenue

GREENWICH BAY

Love Lane

Chepiwanoxet Way

Wolverstone Road

Chepiw

John Wicks
Avenue

P

Chepiwanoxet Point

Potter Road

Cedar Street

Oak Grove Street

Alger Avenue

Bay View   Avenue

N

Spencer Avenue

Division Street

Greenwich

Railroad Tracks

0   miles   1/2

Chepiwanoxet Point, Warwick

In recent years, plastic-bodied jigs have also been very effective. The hot color is chartreuse. Various grubs and fish-like bodies that sport wiggling curly tails have been the best producers.

Whether one uses a bucktail or plastic-bodied jig, fish them deep and slow along sandy bottoms, with occasional jerks of the rod tip. Try to vary the retrieve. In rocky areas, use a float with the jig to keep it above the snags.

D. Pickering

Chepiwanoxet Point, Warwick

Chepiwanoxet Point is a great early season spot.

Directions:

From Route 1 in Warwick, go east (under the railroad tracks), then south (right) 300 yards on Oak Grove Street. Take a left (east) onto Alger Avenue, and follow for 300 yards to the dirt parking area.

This small, undeveloped recreation area has been a popular spring location for many years, but it was recently acquired by the state, assuring continued access. The action at **Chepiwanoxet Point** fades away with the heat of summer, but in the early season schoolie bass, flounder, tautog and some of the first bluefish of the season can be taken. Like Goddard State Park across Greenwich Bay, this is also one of the prime places in the state to try for squeteague from shore. And also like Goddard, it is best fished two hours on either side of high tide. If the baby pogies make an appearance in Greenwich Bay, this can also be a good autumn spot for bass and bluefish.

Poppers For May Blues

This spot offers fishermen the best shot at May bluefish. When fishing a popper there are several variables to consider. The most important are size, color and retrieve. The very best size throughout the Bay is a medium-sized popper that runs about 4 inches and weighs 1 to 1 1/2 ounces, because that simulates a number of baitfish that are found in this area. Sometimes the heavier 2-ounce models work when the fish are less

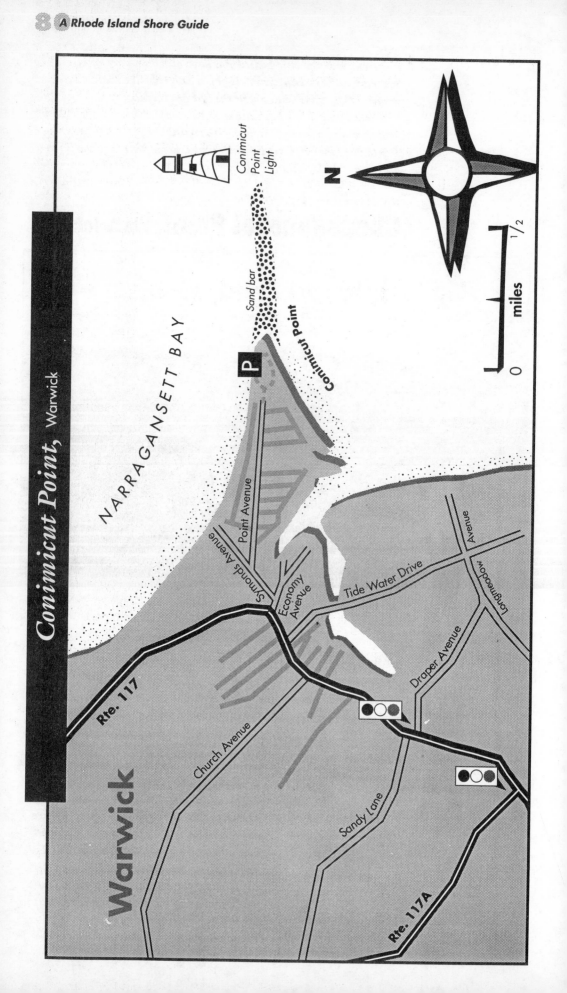

Conimicut Point, Warwick

Conimicut Point Light

Sand bar

Conimicut Point

NARRAGANSETT BAY

N

1/2

0

miles

P

Point Avenue

Symonds Avenue

Economy Avenue

Tide Water Drive

Avenue

Longmeadow

Draper Avenue

Rte. 117

Church Avenue

Warwick

Sandy Lane

Rte. 117A

finicky or when a long cast is needed with heavy gear.

Blues love gaudy colors. In recent years, the bright colors, such as yellow, orange and green, have been hot. If you are making up your own or repainting old plugs, these colors can be used in combination, such as a yellow popper with an orange or red head. One of the best colors in the last few years has been fluorescent orange.

Finally, most fishermen fish a popper too quickly. You want to give a popper just enough pop to keep it on the surface. You may even want to vary your pops, with some coming fast and some slow and far between. If you notice swirls in back of the plug, slow it down a bit but don't stop. Most likely, a hungry fish will come back to hit it.

D. Pickering

Conimicut Point, Warwick

At the end of Conimicut Point the lighthouse is visible in the distance.

Directions:

From Route 117 in Warwick, travel east 110 feet on Economy Avenue, then take a left (north) onto Symonds Avenue. Go 100 yards to Point Road on the right. Follow Point Road east 0.7 mile to the parking area.

Standing on the long sand and gravel bar that extends off **Conimicut Point**, the angler feels that he is standing literally in the middle of Narragansett Bay. Looking north, the skyline of the city of Providence is easily seen, and looking south, the Jamestown and Newport bridges can be seen spanning the two main entrances to the Bay.

This is a very popular spot, attracting fishermen who enjoy everything from bottom fishing for flounder, tautog and scup, to long-distance casters seeking bluefish and stripers, to fly-fishermen who work the shoreline and the bar for schoolies in the spring and fall. In August and September many locals enjoy chunk-bait fishing here all night, and big bluefish and keeper stripers are caught here every year. Care should be taken when wading out on the bar, especially during times of extreme tides.

Conimicut Point is a family-friendly location with plenty of parking and better than average fishing in a semi-urban setting.

These anglers are set up to bottom fish at Conimicut Point.

Rhode Island's Great Bar

No one seem to know just how far you can walk out into Narragansett Bay along Conimicut's great bar at low tide. For sure, many have waded so far out that they could barely see shore. While this opens up a lot of fishing for daring anglers who don a pair of waders in search of stripers, blues and squeteague, be aware of the risks.

The area is known for very strong currents and tides, a plus for fishing, but a danger to wading anglers. Also, the shipping channel lies right in front of this bar. Watch for wakes produced by large boats or even tankers. Many fishermen have been swamped by such wakes. Finally, know the tides you are fishing. On an outgoing tide, you know the water is receding, but be very cautious about incoming tides and keep moving toward the shore as you fish. Be especially careful at times of higher than normal tides, such as in the new moon and full moon phases, and when a strong southerly wind is pushing an incoming tide.

D. Pickering

Providence Hurricane Barrier and River, Providence

Directions:

From Route 195 west, take Exit 2, South Main Street, and go north 300 yards. Take a left onto James Street. Follow James Street 100 yards to South Water Street. Turn south onto South Water Street and proceed 300 yards. Cross Point Street and proceed

The Fox Point Hurricane Barrier was constructed in 1966 to protect downtown Providence from flooding and massive destruction, which the city experienced in the hurricanes of 1938 and 1954. Three huge doors can be lowered, blocking the flow of the Providence River. The water flow through these openings attracts gamefish, and although this area may not be the most aesthetically pleasing place to fish, it can be quite productive. In winter, when cabin fever sets in, anglers come here for the schoolie stripers and white perch that winter over in the river. However, there is a group of urban anglers that does quite well here in the summer and fall casting eels after dark along the barrier, taking some substantial striped bass.

Winter Opportunities

No area of the state offers better winter fishing opportunities in salt water than the Providence River. White perch and striped bass winter-over in the River, lured by the warm waters of the outflows from the Manchester Street power plant. Sometimes these fish are in the river in staggering numbers. Striped bass can be caught with bucktail jigs and various plastic-bodied jigs by working them along the bottom with light tackle. Be sure to use a slow retrieve and

The doors of the Hurricane Barrier open, drawing fish to the water flow.

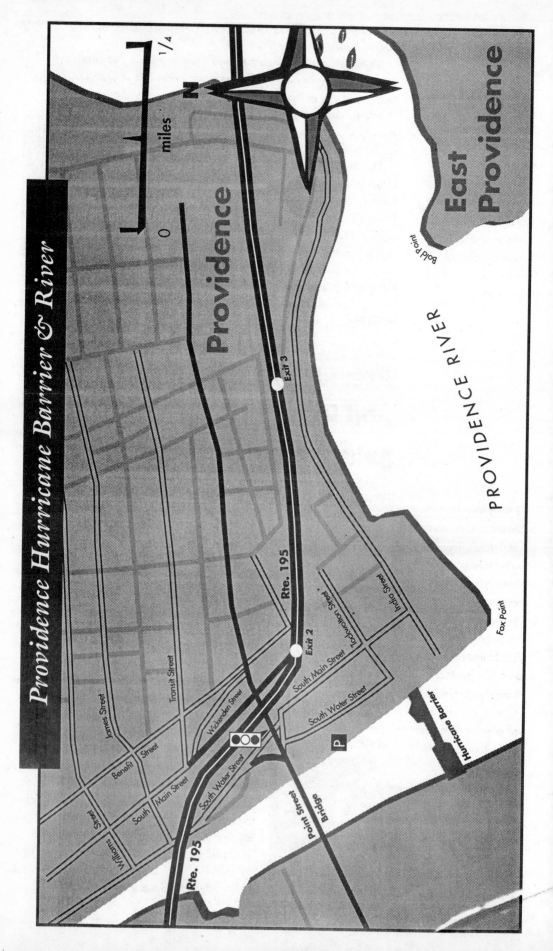

Providence Hurricane Barrier & River

East Providence

Providence

PROVIDENCE RIVER

Bold Point

Fox Point

miles

¼

0

N

Exit 3

Rte. 195

Exit 2

India Street

Brook Street

Tockwatton Street

South Main Street

South Water Street

James Street

Transit Street

Wickenden Street

Benefit Street

South Main Street

South Water Street

Williams Street

South

Rte. 195

Point Street Bridge

Hurricane Barrier

P

onto the onramp for Route 195 east. Bear right almost immediately off the ramp onto South Main Street. Follow South Main Street south for 200 yards to Tockwotton Street. Take a right onto Tockwotton and follow for 100 yards, then go right onto South Water Street. Parking is available on the street.

expect hits to be soft due to the cold water, which slows the bass' metabolism.

White perch will travel in large schools. They prefer very small bucktail jigs (1/8 ounce) as well as tiny, 1-inch plastic-bodied shads and tubes. Light colors are best.

D. Pickering

The city is visible from the paths alongside the Providence River.

Bold Point, East Providence

Directions:

From Route 195 in East Providence, take the Veteran's Memorial Parkway exit, and proceed south on Veteran's Memorial Parkway 0.5 mile to First Street. Turn right onto First Street and follow for one block to Mauran Avenue. Turn left onto Mauran Avenue, go over the railroad tracks, and then take a left onto Pier Road. Follow Pier Road 0.5 mile to the park and a parking area on the right adjacent to a boat launch ramp and pier.

Next to this small park is the narrow entrance to the Seekonk River, one of the major rivers feeding into Narragansett Bay. The current sweeps around Bold Point and good fishable water is a short cast from shore, so fly-rodders and bottom-dunkers alike do well here. This is especially true in the late season when the upper Bay holds small bait, like immature menhaden and silversides. There are also doormat-sized fluke taken here on occasion. Casting live eels after dark is popular in September and October.

The quality of the fishing, however, is quite variable due to the influence of the river, which can flush a huge amount of fresh and brackish water into the Bay after a few days of rain. Although it is not as well known a winter fishery as nearby Providence River, fishermen report good catches of small striped bass and white perch in January and February.

Tricks With Plastics

Soft plastic fish-like lures, 4 to 5 inches in length and light in color, have been the hottest lures here in recent years for striped bass. To fish the moving waters on the river side of Bold Point, mount these lures on barbed jigheads weighing 1/4 to 1 ounce. Cast crosscurrent, allow the lure to drop down near the bottom, and jig in with upward strokes of the rod. Most hits will

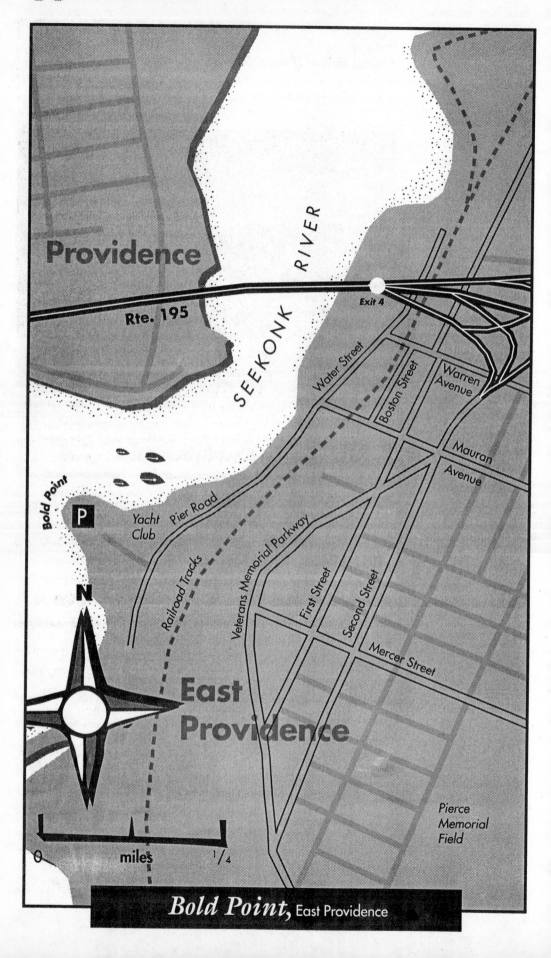

Providence

SEEKONK RIVER

Rte. 195

Exit 4

Water Street

Boston Street

Warren Avenue

Mauran Avenue

Bold Point

P

Yacht Club

Pier Road

Railroad Tracks

Veterans Memorial Parkway

First Street

Second Street

Mercer Street

N

East Providence

Pierce Memorial Field

0   miles   1/4

Bold Point, East Providence

From Bold Point Providence is to the north.

come as the jig is dropping down.

Along the structure of the west side of the Point, you can also use these lures, but rig them differently. In this area you want to fish the surface. Thread the plastic bodies on barbed worm hooks in sizes 3/0 to 5/0. These lightweight surface darters are cast with light spinning tackle and fished with a twitching motion of the rod tip, which drives finicky bass wild. The larger-sized plastic bodies are more effective for surface applications because they have a little more weight and are easier to cast, but don't use so much weight that they sink quickly.

D. Pickering

East Providence Bike Path, East Providence

Directions:

From the intersection of Route 103 and Veteran's Memorial Parkway in East Providence, follow Veteran's Memorial Parkway 2.7 miles to the parking area on the left, across from Metacomet Golf Club.

The view across the Providence River may leave a bit to be desired—the oil and natural gas tanks on the opposite shore—but fishing from the rocks along the Bike Path is both popular and productive. The paved path follows the abandoned tracks of the New York, New Haven and Hartford Railroad and access is easy.

Families come here during the day in the summer to fish for scup, fluke and snapper blues, and the nighttime crowd casts along the rocks for stripers and bluefish, which tend to show up when the baitfish schools move into the upper Bay.

There's plenty of room to spread out, but many fishermen prefer the area from the opening of Watchemoket Cove down to Kettle Point where the remains of old piers hold bait. Chunk fishing with cut herring or menhaden can produce some big stripers in the fall, but be

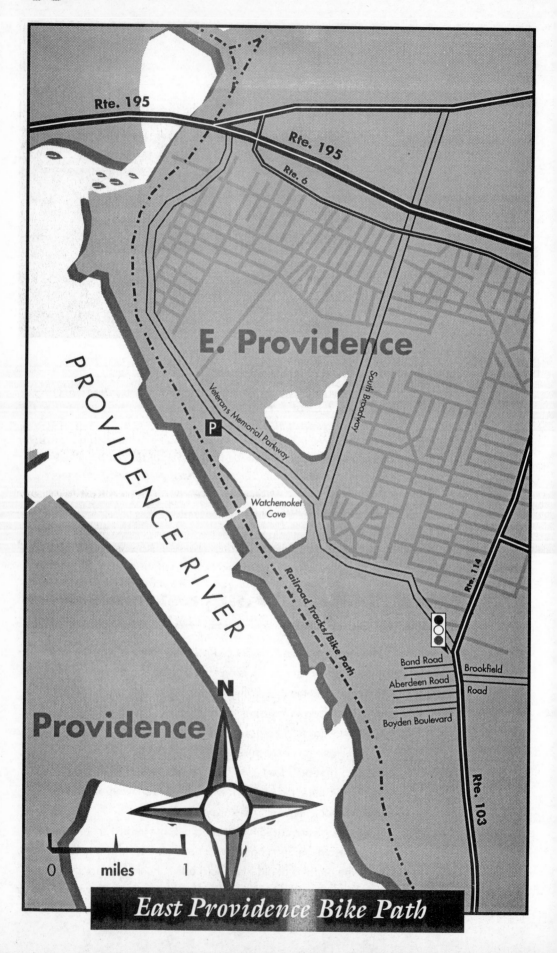

Rte. 195

Rte. 195

Rte. 6

E. Providence

P R O V I D E N C E   R I V E R

PROVIDENCE

Veterans Memorial Parkway

South Broadway

P

Watchemoket Cove

Railroad Tracks/Bike Path

N

Providence

Bond Road

Aberdeen Road

Boyden Boulevard

Brookfield Road

Rte. 114

Rte. 103

0   miles   1

East Providence Bike Path

The Providence skyline can be seen north of the bike path.

sure to bring along plenty of terminal tackle, as the bottom is covered with snags.

One word of caution: Be sure to keep a sharp eye out for bike traffic as you're walking. This is a very popular route and some of the bicyclists here seem to think they're competing in the Tour de France!

Canal Bikes Work Here, Too

With miles of access along the East Providence Bike Path, it makes sense to use a bike to travel to fishing locations. Like fishermen at the Cape Cod Canal, Rhode Island bikers who fish this area also rig their bikes with rod holders, baskets and headlights. Rod holders can be simply made out of PVC piping that is clamped or taped to rear supports on your bike. I like to carry at least two rod holders. Baskets are handy to carry tackle, food and extra clothing. Headlights are a must if you plan to fish along here after dark. Finally, take a bike lock along and use it if you plan to fish a distance from your bike. Using a bike is a great way to make access easier and give you more mobility in areas like this.

D. Pickering

The long shoreline at the East Providence Bike Path is a popular bottom-fishing location.

These anglers try their luck in Watchemoket Cove, which is easily accessible from the bike path.

Barrington Beach, **Barrington**

Bluefish often push bait up to Barrington Beach in the fall.

Directions:

From the intersection of Routes 114 and 103 and Rumstock Road in Barrington, follow Rumstock Road south 0.8 mile to Chachapacasset Road on the right. Follow Chachapacasset Road west 0.5 mile to the end (Bay Road). Turn left onto Bay Road and follow to the beach parking area.

A southwest-facing shore where the prevailing breezes of the summer and fall push in warm water and baitfish, **Barrington Beach** is a spot for any style of fishing. This is a very popular bathing beach and as such is not a good choice for fishing on a bright summer day, but in the early morning and especially in the evening the fishermen take over.

Bluefish often blitz this beach in the fall, but stripers can be caught here too if you fish after dark. Try casting flies or small jigs along the grass banks on the eastern end of the beach, or continue wading and casting your way out to Rumstick Point, which is the western side of the entrance to the Warren River.

The best feature of this location may be the easy access with parking nearby, making it a great spot for anglers who are unable to walk a long distance or for young fishermen.

Bluefish Blitz

This stretch of beach has been the most consistent place to find a bluefish blitz in Narragansett Bay in recent years. The best action will occur from late August through mid October, with the month of September being prime time. Southwest winds will drive massive schools of peanut bunker to this bowl-shaped beach, setting up an ideal ambush site and some of the wildest action imaginable.

Anglers often search the waters for the trigger mechanisms that set a blitz in motion. Look for diving gulls and schools of bait, which resemble dark clouds on the surface. Though a blitz can occur anytime, your best chance of finding one is during

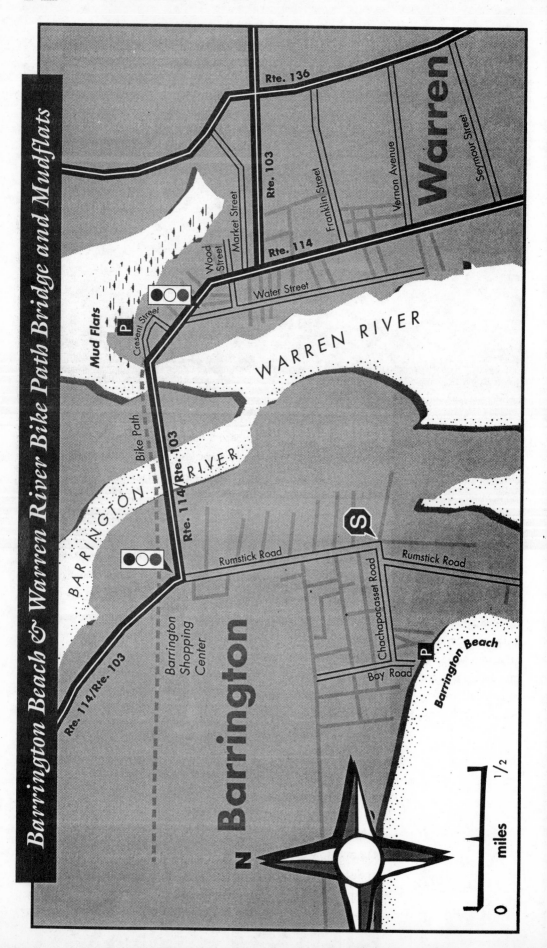

Barrington Beach & Warren River Bike Path Bridge and Mudflats

Warren

Rte. 136

Rte. 103

Franklin Street

Vernon Avenue

Seymour Street

Rte. 114

Market Street

Wood Street

Water Street

Mud Flats

Cresent Street

P

WARREN RIVER

Bike Path

Rte. 114/Rte. 103

BARRINGTON RIVER

Rumstick Road

Rumstick Road

Barrington Shopping Center

Chachapacasset Road

Barrington

Bay Road

Barrington Beach

P

S

Rte. 114/Rte. 103

N

0 miles ½

times of low light, such as early morning, evening and on cloudy days. In a blitz with large areas of breaking fish in front of you, try to cast on the perimeter of the schools of blues. Casting right into thousands of frenzied fish often results in cut line and lost plugs.

D. Pickering

Warren River Bike Path Bridge and Mudflats, Warren

Mudflats and marsh are north of the Warren River Bike Path.

Directions:

From the intersection where Route 114 joins Route 103 in Warren, proceed northwest 0.4 mile to Crescent Street on the right (last street before the bridge). Park on Crescent Street and walk down the bike path to the bridge.

Although there isn't much room to fish here, at least on the bridge itself, this spot attracts many bait-fishing enthusiasts who come here in the spring and fall to try for big stripers. This is no surprise because herring move through in the early season and there are often menhaden around from the end of August right through autumn.

The Warren River Bike Path Bridge and Mudflats is a choke point between the Barrington and Warren rivers with a fast current flow, so it is best fished on an incoming tide when your bait will be pushed away from the bridge pilings. There is a marsh bordering the northeast side of the bridge and this is the place to go if you prefer casting to bottom fishing.

If you wade off the edge of the marsh, be careful of stepping into the deep river channel that is close to shore. The mudflats farther inside the Barrington River are a popular area for wading and fly-fishing, but they are well named and the footing can be very soft.

Many Ways To Fish Herring

Most fishermen who line this bridge in late spring will fish herring or alewives on an incoming tide in a variety of ways to catch keeper bass. Some will opt to use them live, ferrying live ones in buckets from their

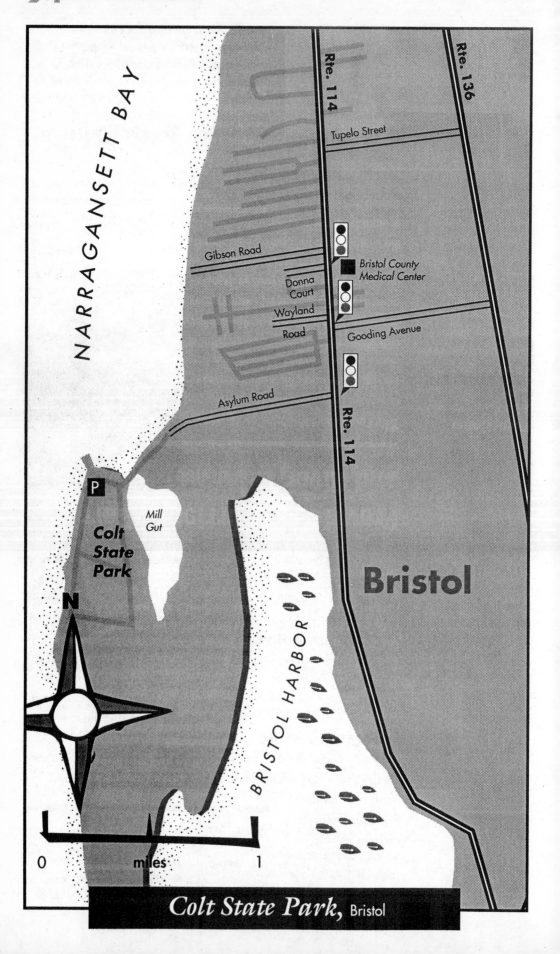

NARRAGANSETT BAY

Rte. 114

Rte. 136

Tupelo Street

Gibson Road

Bristol County
Medical Center

Donna
Court

Wayland

Road

Gooding Avenue

Asylum Road

Rte. 114

P

Mill
Gut

Colt
State
Park

Bristol

N

BRISTOL HARBOR

0   miles   1

Colt State Park, Bristol

parked trucks that have large livewells inside. Live ones can be fished weightless, with just a hook through the nose of the herring, or on a fishfinder rig with added weight to bring the bait down.

An easier way is to use dead herring, which can be easily stored in a small cooler with ice. Dead ones should be used on a fishfinder rig with the hook passing under the chin and up through the roof of the head. Dead herring work especially well in areas of current that impart action to the dead fish. Use enough sinker weight to get the bait on or near the bottom.

Another way to use dead herring is to chunk them. An average-sized herring can be sliced into two or three chunks. The head and midsections work the best. A chunk should also be used with a fishfinder rig or with a sliding egg sinker.

D. Pickering

Colt State Park, Bristol

Mill Gut empties into the Bay at Colt State Park.

Directions:

From Route 114 in Bristol, follow Asylum Road 0.7 mile to Colt Drive and the park entrance. Parking is available at North Point parking area near Mill Gut Bridge and throughout the park.

Colt State Park, like Goddard State Park across Narragansett Bay, was once a grand estate. Colonel Samuel P. Colt, nephew of Samuel Colt of revolver fame, opened his 464-acre farm in 1905 for the purpose of breeding prize-winning cattle. From the beginning, the farm welcomed the public, which came to marvel at the expansive lawns, sculptures and luxurious accommodations for Col. Colt and his livestock alike. The State of Rhode Island took over the estate in 1965 and Colt State Park was opened soon afterward.

Today many people in the Rhode Island feel that Colt is the most

These anglers are trying their luck plugging off the rocks at Colt State Park.

beautiful park in the state. But beyond it's beauty, the park offers many options for recreation, and one of the best is fishing. With over a mile of shorefront, anglers can always find a place to cast, and with acres of rolling lawns, hiking and biking trails and hundreds of picnic tables, all members of the family will be able to find some outdoor activity to fill the day.

The best season-long option here is bait fishing for scup and fluke, but the deepwater channel outside the Mill Gut Bridge holds stripers and bluefish in the fall. Mill Gut, a large salt pond near the entrance to the park, is a great place to fly-fish for schoolies.

The only negative aspect to fishing Colt State Park is the park's hours of operation—sunrise to sunset. This precludes fishing after dark, which most hardcore striper and weakfish anglers would prefer. But being at the gate at sunrise will allow you to get in an hour or so of good striper fishing at a beautiful location, and bluefish often chase bait along these shores in the early evening.

Mill Gut Bridge spans the narrow opening into the Bay.

The Wonders of the Colt Farm

Visitors to Colt State Park can't help but notice as they approach the entrance to the park the impressive marble walls topped by two huge statues of Jersey bulls. The marble wall is inscribed, "Colt Farm, Private Property, Public Welcome." In the early part of the twentieth century, Colonel Samuel Colt's farm was known far and wide. Visitors, guided through the huge stone barn by workers in white suits, marveled at the Jersey cattle, whose horns were polished and tails cleaned every day, and the spotless barn itself, which was heated in the winter and had a polished mirror-like tile ceiling to reflect the images of the Colonel's prized livestock. The Colonel encouraged local families to visit, and many would come in the summer to dig clams in Mill Gut and fish for flounder, tautog and striped bass.

G. Bourque

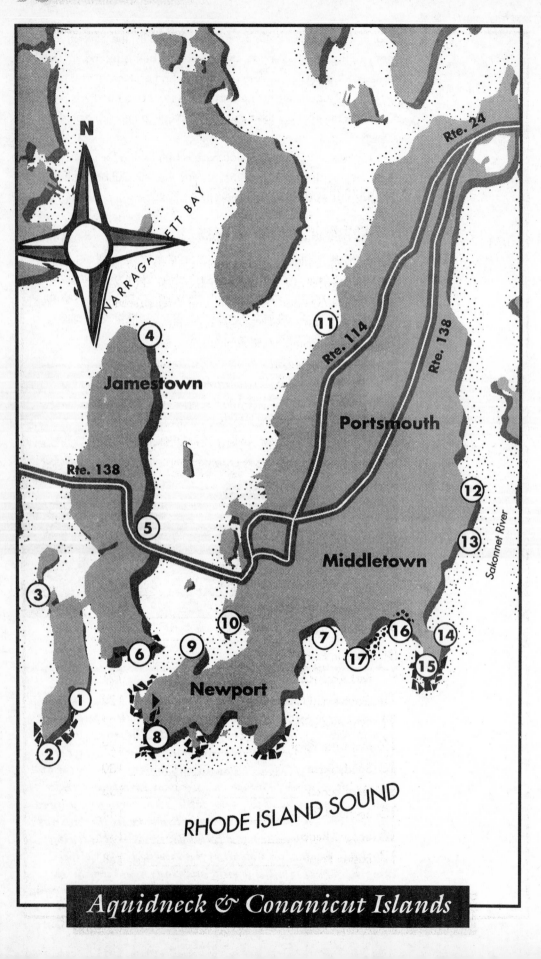

Aquidneck & Conanicut Islands

Aquidneck Island
Conanicut Island

The two largest islands at the entrance to Narragansett Bay are **Aquidneck**, containing the towns of Newport, Middletown and Portsmouth, and **Conanicut** (Jamestown). The city of Newport is internationally famous for its sailing, music festivals, millionaires' mansions, and trendy downtown shopping and restaurant district, but nearby Brenton Point State Park, Sachuest Point National Wildlife Refuge in neighboring Middletown, and Beavertail State Park over the Newport Bridge in Jamestown, are wild and beautiful places. And all these spots frequently have great fishing.

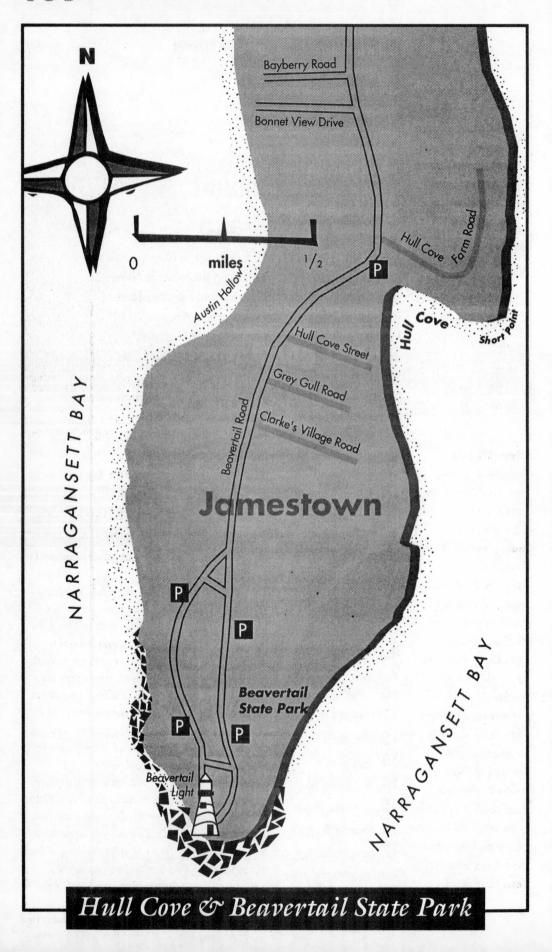

N

NARRAGANSETT BAY

0   miles   1/2

Bayberry Road

Bonnet View Drive

Hull Cove Farm Road

P

Austin Hollow

Hull Cove

Short Point

Hull Cove Street

Grey Gull Road

Clarke's Village Road

Beavertail Road

Jamestown

P

P

Beavertail State Park

P

P

NARRAGANSETT BAY

Beavertail Light

Hull Cove & Beavertail State Park

Hull Cove, Jamestown

To the east of the rocky beach at Hull Cove is Short Point.

Directions:

From the downtown waterfront area in the town of Jamestown, follow Conanicus Avenue south into Walcott Avenue. Follow Walcott Avenue south 1/8 mile to Hamilton Avenue on the right. Follow Hamilton Avenue west for 1 mile. Just after Mackerel Cove Beach at the entrance to Fort Getty Recreation Area, the road becomes Beaver Tail Road. Follow Beaver Tail Road south 1 1/2 miles to the small public access parking area on the left, just after Hull Cove Farm Road.

After a 300-yard walk down a muddy path through the bushes, the angler is rewarded with the rocky beachfront of **Hull Cove**. This area is often passed up by fishermen heading out to Beavertail State Park, and that may be a mistake. A southerly swell pushes bait into this cove, and stripers and bluefish can be taken quite close to shore with less of the danger inherent in climbing around the rocks at Beavertail. A few days of hard southwest wind can also push in quite a bit of weed, however. Some fishermen prefer to walk around the cove to the east and fish the rocks off Short Point. Not only is this a good bluefish and striper spot, but some very nice tautog are taken here in spring, too.

Dead Eel Tricks

Many fishermen who sling live eels keep their dead ones after a night of eel fishing since dead eels work just as well as live ones in a good-sized surf. After getting home from fishing, place the dead ones in a plastic bag and freeze them. When going fishing again, take the bagged dead ones and thaw them out. The trick is to stretch the eel out before using it since the freezing process compresses the eel's backbone. Simply grab the head and the tail and pull.

Now you are ready to hook and fish your dead eel just like you would a live one. Other fishermen may choose to rig their dead eels before freezing. Rigging may be done with wobble plates up front or by threading a line through the eel and attaching a hook up front and in the rear. However one chooses to fish or rig a dead eel, they do work!

D. Pickering

Anglers fish off the rocks in front of Beavertail Lighthouse.

Beavertail State Park, Jamestown

This is the terrain you'll encounter in front of the lighthouse at Beavertail State Park.

Directions:

From the downtown waterfront area in the town of Jamestown, follow Conanicus Avenue south into Walcott Avenue. Follow Walcott Avenue south 1/8 mile to Hamilton Avenue on the right. Follow Hamilton Avenue west for 1 mile. Just after Mackerel Cove Beach, at the entrance to Fort Getty Recreation Area, the road becomes Beavertail Road. Follow Beavertail Road south 2 1/4 miles to the park entrance. Parking areas are on the west

Nighttime fishing on the rocks under the light at Beaver Tail or on a hazy morning as the sun rises is an unforgettable experience. One of the most popular and challenging locations for the hardcore Rhody surfcasting crowd, trophy-sized stripers and bluefish are taken at **Beavertail State Park** every year. Casting off the rocks (and landing a big fish!) is not for the faint of heart. It's important to have a game plan in place before you make your way to the water's edge. Safety equipment, such as studded-soled creepers, is a necessity, and it's not a bad idea to wear a self-inflating personal floatation device, too. Many of the rock ledges are smooth shale, covered with a green-brown slime that makes walking seem more like ice-skating. If a large ocean swell is running, it is best to fish on either side of the point.

Try casting large wooden surface plugs in the wash around the boulders or swimming a live eel near the drop-offs next to the ledges. Very large striped bass are

History Adds to the Surf Casting Mystique

The point at Beavertail has been the location of a lighthouse for almost 250 years. In Colonial times Narragansett Bay was one of the most important deep-water, protected anchorages in the world, and it was vital that ships be warned away from the reefs and rips at the western entrance of the Bay. British troops, retreating from

and east sides of the park along the circular park road, with limited parking near the lighthouse.

often taken here right next to the shore, so be sure to fish your lure or bait all the way in.

There are so many shelves, ledges and other structure to explore here that it makes no sense to restrict yourself to one spot. If a prime casting location is taken, there is sure to be another nearby. Move around, read the water and the chances are good that you'll connect with a substantial striper or bluefish, especially in the fall when the southerly gamefish migration is in full swing.

Beavertail is wild and beautiful and for many fishermen is the essence of fishing Rhode Island's rocky shores.

Newport in 1779, burned the (then wooden) structure, and it was rebuilt in 1783. In 1856 the stone and brick structure was constructed that stands today. The light was automated in 1972 and it still guides fishermen, pleasure boaters and commercial craft to safe harbor. To stand on the rocks below the sweeping light as the fog horn blares and cast into the churning waves is a quintessential Rhode Island surf-fishing experience.

G. Bourque

Beavertail Light is the third oldest lighthouse in the country.

Fort Getty Recreation Area,
Jamestown

Directions:

From the downtown waterfront area of the town of Jamestown, follow Conanicus Avenue south into Walcott Avenue. Follow Walcott Avenue south 1/8 mile to Hamilton Avenue on the right. Follow Hamilton Avenue west for 1 mile, past Mackerel Cove Beach, to the park entrance on the right.

Just about any fishing style can be practiced here, from bottom dunking for scup to fly-fishing for stripers and weakfish, to surf casting off a rocky beach for bluefish. There is also a large seasonal camping area, catering primarily to the trailer and recreational-vehicle crowd, many of whom set up their rigs for the summer on the bluff in the center of the park. On the northern end of the area is a dock that is used by bait fishermen to catch scup in the summer and flounder in the spring and fall, but this dock is also worth the attention of plug casters. This is because the channel between the end of the dock and Dutch Island to the north has a good tidal flow, and stripers (and occasionally weakfish) feed here in the spring and summer after dark.

To the east of the bluff and the trailer village is a large marsh that empties into Dutch Island Harbor. Schoolie stripers and weakfish can be found off the entrance of the marsh, especially on a dropping tide. Fly-fishermen like this location because they are protected from the predominantly southwest wind.

On the opposite side of the bluff, near the entrance to the camping area, is a parking area near a picnic pavilion. Park here and fish anywhere along the outer cobblestone beach or rocks in either direction. This is plug-fishing territory and schools of bluefish sometimes push bait right up on these rocks. This is also a great spot to cast live eels after dark or at first light.

Camping and Bluefish

For $20 a night if you are going to use a tent or $25 a night for an RV site, you can camp at Fort Getty. Reservations, made at least a month in advance, are recommended. The season is from May 20 to October 1. It is one heck of a bargain, particularly for the traveling fisherman. By all accounts, the atmosphere at the camp is one of friendship and camaraderie, and many people return each year. I wish there were more spots like this in places not so close to my home.

Once camped at Fort Getty, the striped bass world is your oyster. You are now in the center of striped bass fisherman's heaven, Jamestown, Rhode Island. From Fort Getty it is only a short ride to Beavertail or Newport, or Rhody's south shore. If you decide you do not want to leave the camp—as many do—there is often good fishing right

The view north out of Fox Hill Salt Marsh will attract the fisherman's interest.

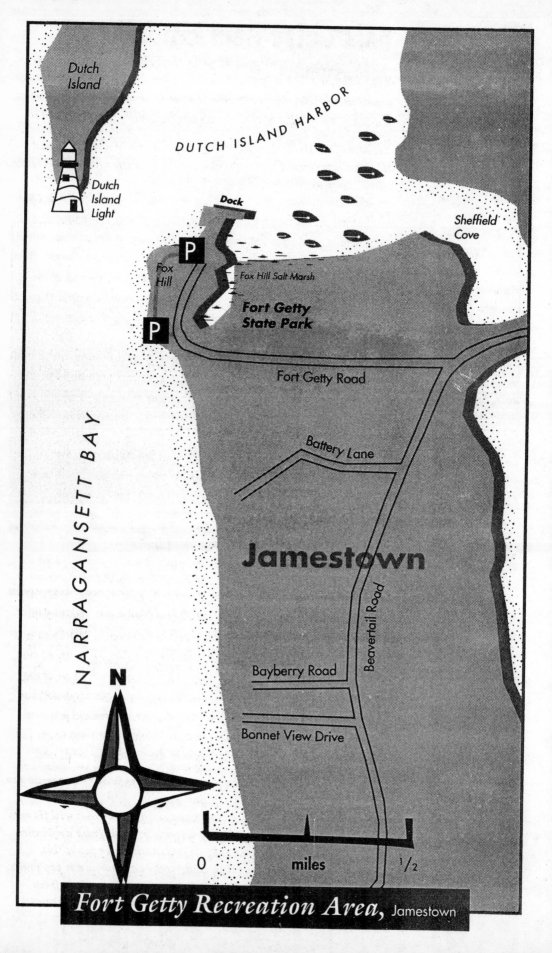

Dutch Island

DUTCH ISLAND HARBOR

Dutch Island Light

Sheffield Cove

Dock

P

Fox Hill

Fox Hill Salt Marsh

Fort Getty State Park

P

Fort Getty Road

Battery Lane

Jamestown

Beavertail Road

Bayberry Road

Bonnet View Drive

NARRAGANSETT BAY

N

0   miles   1/2

Fort Getty Recreation Area, Jamestown

off the camp dock and also where Sheffield Cove flows into Dutch Harbor.

Each August, something spawns in Sheffield Cove. I'm not sure what it is, just that it brings in the bluefish. For a couple weeks there is sporadic action from good-sized bluefish. When it happens, it's the worst-kept secret in Jamestown. The feisty bluefish are great sport, particularly for light-tackle and fly-rod fishermen. In the late fall, usually after Thanksgiving, there is a good run of mackerel, and don't be surprised if you run into some late-season slammer bluefish at this time as well.

J. Lyons

The dock at Fort Getty Recreation Area offers good pier fishing.

Park Dock, Jamestown

Directions:

From the waterfront downtown area of the town of Jamestown, follow Conanicus Avenue north 1.2 miles, under the Route 138 access road to the Newport Bridge. At the stop sign, continue north on East Shore Road for 3.4 miles to Broad Street on the right. Follow Broad Street 100 yards to the small parking area.

Park Dock isn't really a dock at all, just the remains of a broken-down jetty and a small, public, sand and gravel beach. Park Dock is a favorite place for local residents to take their families for a day at the beach and some fishing. This is a great family spot, with views of the boat traffic going in and out of Newport and down Narragansett Bay. In the spring, flounder and tautog can be caught off the old jetty and beach, and in the summer, scup are easy to find in the deep water just off the beach. The area is protected from the prevailing winds and ocean waves, and is a great spot for setting up some light rods with squid strips or clam necks for bait and catching a bunch of scup for dinner.

Handy Bait Bucket

A very handy bait bucket that will fit onto your surf belt can be made from a cylindrical baby wipes container. To make this bucket, first rivet (use aluminum pop rivets and backup plates) two loops made from nylon strapping to the top of the container.

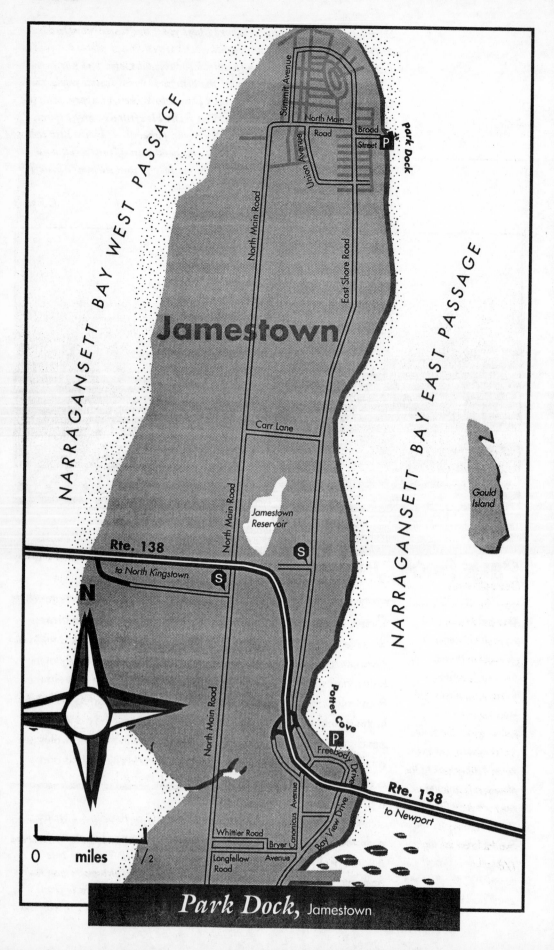

NARRAGANSETT BAY WEST PASSAGE

NARRAGANSETT BAY EAST PASSAGE

Summit Avenue

North Main Road

Union Avenue

Broad Street

park Dock

P

East Shore Road

North Main Road

Jamestown

Carr Lane

North Main Road

Jamestown Reservoir

S

Gould Island

Rte. 138

to North Kingstown

S

N

Potter Cove

P

Freebody Drive

Rte. 138

to Newport

Canonicus Avenue

Bryer

Bay View Drive

Whittier Road

Longfellow Road

Avenue

0   miles   1/2

Park Dock, Jamestown

These loops will form the holders to pass your surf belt through. Next, drill a hole through the cover of the container and a hole through the side of the container. The holes should be the diameter of a small piece of rope that will be knotted into place to keep the cover secure. Lastly, drill holes in the bottom for drainage. The container allows for mobility when fishing chunks, eels or seaworms.

D. Pickering

Looking east from Park Dock, you can seel across Narragansett Bay.

Potter Cove, Jamestown

Directions:

From the waterfront downtown area of the town of Jamestown, proceed north on Conanicus Avenue 3/10 mile. Bear right onto Bayview Drive. Follow Bayview Drive 6/10 mile, under the Route 138 access to the Newport Bridge, then bear left onto Freebody Drive. Parking is available on the right, 1/8 mile.

Potter Cove is a great destination for the fly or light-tackle fisherman who wants to wade and fish over a flat, sand and gravel bottom. Although this is primarily an early or late season spot (because the water over the shallows warms too much at the height of the season), the action can be quite good at first light or in the evening when stripers move in to feed on the abundant silversides.

In recent years, schools of baby bunker (menhaden) have moved in and out of the cove in the fall, setting up some good fishing for medium-sized bluefish and, on occasion, bonito and false albacore. This is an easy, relaxing place to wade fish, protected from the predominantly southwest wind, without the hazards of the rocky shelves elsewhere on Conanicut Island.

The rocks that border the east end of the cove at Taylor Point are a good spot to bottom fish for flounder in the early season and scup all summer long.

Take Your Pick
Potter Cove, a municipal access area by the Newport Bridge, just may be Jamestown's most versatile public access area

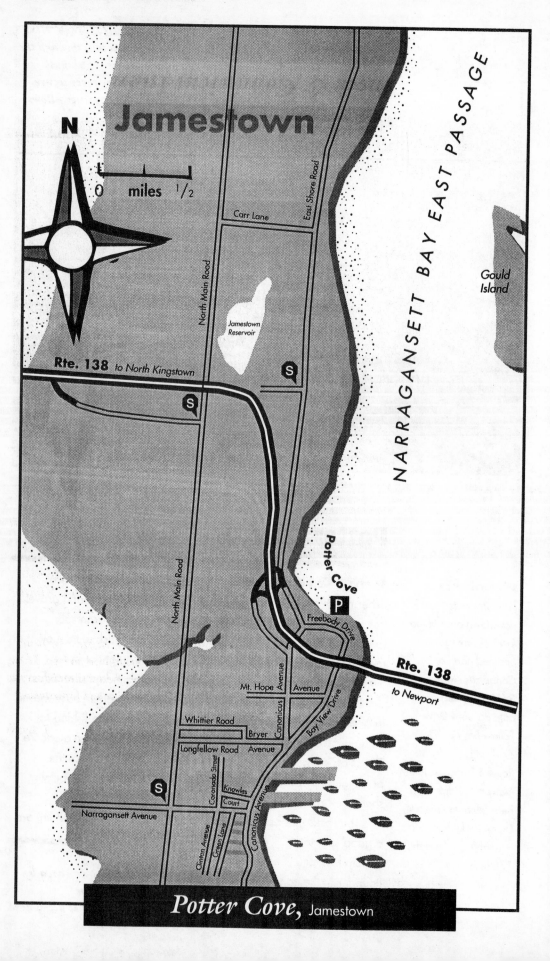

N

Jamestown

0 miles 1/2

Carr Lane

East Shore Road

NARRAGANSETT BAY EAST PASSAGE

Gould Island

North Main Road

Jamestown Reservoir

Rte. 138 *to North Kingstown*

Potter Cove

P

Freebody Drive

Rte. 138

to Newport

Mt. Hope Avenue

Avenue

Canonicus Avenue

Boy View Drive

Whittier Road

Bryer

Longfellow Road Avenue

Clinton Avenue

Coronado Street

Green Lane

Knowlas Court

Canonicus Avenue

Narragansett Avenue

Potter Cove, Jamestown

Potter Cove is easily waded and is protected from the wind most of the time.

for the shore-bound fisherman.

Bait fishermen frequent the area in pursuit of blackfish. Spin fishermen like to plug the area with topwater lures, particularly late in the day during the warm-weather months. But the area's most rabid enthusiasts are the fly-fishermen. Drive by Potter Cove any late afternoon during the fishing season and you will most likely see a fly-fisherman's reflection shimmering across the tranquil waters of the flats.

Fly-fishermen like to have options and Potter Cove provides a bevy of them. There are currents sweeping towards the rocks within an easy cast, providing opportunities for dead drifting a Glass Minnow or bouncing a Clouser. There are large wading flats that offer excellent topwater action with poppers and sliders.

In the spring, school stripers provide fast action in May. In June, big stripers cruise the shallows searching for crabs and shrimp. Later, in the summer, bonito and false albacore make forays into the cove to feast upon the massive schools of silversides that invade Jamestown's waters each summer. Potter's is a gem.

J. Lyons

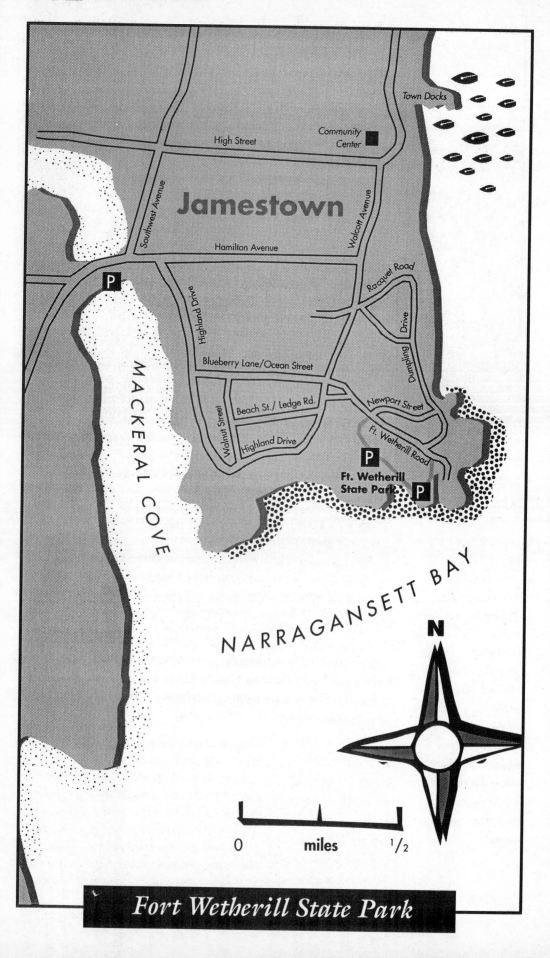

Jamestown

Town Docks

High Street

Community Center

Southwest Avenue

Walcott Avenue

Hamilton Avenue

P

Racquet Road

Highland Drive

Drive

Dumpling

Blueberry Lane/Ocean Street

MACKERAL COVE

Beach St./ Ledge Rd.

Newport Street

Walnut Street

Ft. Wetherill Road

Highland Drive

P

Ft. Wetherill
State Park

P

NARRAGANSETT BAY

N

0   miles   1/2

Fort Wetherill State Park

Fort Wetherill State Park,
Jamestown

Castle Hill Lighthouse in Newport is visible from Fort Wetherill State Park.

Directions:

From the downtown waterfront area of the town of Jamestown, follow Conanicus Avenue south into Walcott Avenue, then south 6/10 mile to Fort Wetherill Road on the left. Follow Fort Wetherill Road southeast 1/4 mile to the state park entrance on the right. Enter the park and bear left. Follow this road 1/8 mile to the parking area at the public boat ramp.

Fort Wetherill was part of the extensive coastal defenses that guarded the entrance to Narragansett Bay and the deep-water harbor at nearby Newport. Part of the fort area is presently being restored for use as an information and interpretive center. There are two coves adjacent to the area being restored that offer good fishing, although the areas are quite small. Both have rocky beaches where stripers search for food after dark in the shallow water, and the rocky point between the coves fishes well for bluefish and stripers if you use a stout rod capable of lifting the fish up the rocks. Inside the restoration area of the fort is a steel bulkhead that is a favorite spot to bottom fish for blackfish (tautog) and flounder in the early season and scup all summer long.

An adventurous angler, properly equipped with studded boots or waders, may want to explore the rocky outcroppings west of the cove because big stripers can be found in the white water at

Rocks and Tautog at the Fort
Fort Wetherill State Park is known as an exceptionally good place for diving and has become Rhode Island's scuba headquarters. Many of the divers are spear fishermen, and if you have any doubts about the presence of fish at the fort, they will be dispelled after you see a diver come out of the water with a bag full of fish.
Not only stripers and blues, but also big

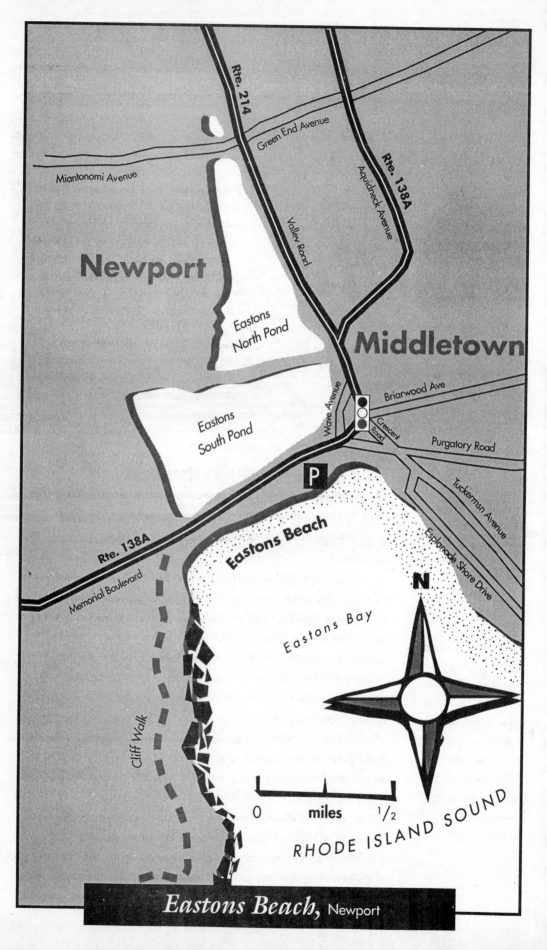

Eastons Beach, Newport

the base of the rocks, but extreme care should be taken here, especially when there is big surf.

The abandoned gun emplacements, observation points and bunkers are a cool place to wander around and explore, regardless of your fishing success, and the state park lawns and picnic areas make this a good place to take the non-fishing members of the family.

tautog and flounder are present. Tautog, also known as blackfish, make an exceptional meal; the mild white meat is firm and flaky and only slightly grainy. Blackfish are caught on bait, usually live green crabs, fished on the bottom.

Fort Wetherill is a Rhode Island Department of Environmental Management area, consisting of hiking trails, picnicking facilities, as well as the abandoned fortifications used for the defense of Narragansett Bay during World War II. The 61-acre park affords some lovely views of Newport Harbor and the East Passage from atop the park's 100-foot granite cliffs.

If you are looking for a fishing spot that will keep the non-fishing members of the family happy, as well as providing creature-comforts like restrooms and picnic tables, this spot is a good pick.

J. Lyons

Eastons Beach, Newport

Directions:
From downtown Newport, follow Route 138A (Memorial Boulevard) northeast 1 mile to the beach.

Also known as First Beach, **Eastons Beach** can have fantastic fishing at times but at others, including for most of the summer, it can be unfishable.

In the early season, light-tackle and fly-fishermen consider this a required stop in the search for the first striped bass arriving from points south. The key is to fish the edges, either the west end below the beginning of the famous Cliff Walk, or the east end and the rocky shore out toward Easton Point. The middle part of the 3/4-mile-long beach will have blitzing, early season bluefish on occasion.

In the summer, however, most experienced fishermen will utilize Eastons Beach parking lot to leave their cars and head down the Cliff Walk to better fishing. The problem with fishing the beach area itself is the presence of a thick mat of clinging, red seaweed that at times makes even swimming along most of the beach impossible. Your best bet is the eastern end, which seems to collect less weed.

In the fall, the weed tends to clear out enough for decent fishing, especially if Mother Nature provides a few strong passing cold fronts with strong northeast winds to move the weed away. The cooler water tends to turn the fish on, too, and roving schools of false albacore sometimes sweep along this beach, giving the shore-bound angler a rare shot at these speedy gamefish.

The beginning of Newport's famous Cliff Walk can be seen from Eastons Beach.

Fall Blitz

Fall fishing at Newport's First Beach during the migration can be excellent. For several weeks at the close of the 2000 fishing season, peanut bunker, striped bass and gorilla bluefish all came together to make for a memorable close to what was already a great season. Even with the presence of thick seaweed, the massive schools of gamefish afforded anglers action that was furious. For a time, surfcasters were given easy pickings and forgot just how difficult fishing is usually. It's the challenge we profess to love, but oh, it is nice to have it easy once in a while.

The eastern end of the beach is sometimes a better bet when the red seaweed rolls in.

For weeks the action continued. Anglers commented that sometimes the fish were so close, they appeared to be in an aquarium. The fish keyed in on bunker that seemed to increase in numbers as time went on, treating the anglers to seldom-seen displays of feeding behavior. For a while, the mystery of surfcasting was solved, and all seemed perfectly logical and predictable. Every afternoon around 4:30 the fish would be at First Beach. In the middle of the day they would be at Second or Third Beach, but always hovering close to the shore.

In late October and into early November patterns began to change. The keepers that had been regularly leaving the beach by their gill plates, started to dwindle. Smaller fish appeared in greater numbers and the anglers scaled down their tackle to accommodate them. Then it was over. The bait, and with it our migrating quarry, moved on.

J. Lyons

Brenton Point, Newport

Rocks make fishing Brenton Point both productive and dangerous.

Directions:

From Route 138A in downtown Newport, follow Bellevue Avenue south 1 3/4 miles, then west for 1/4 mile. Travel north 1/8 mile on Coggeshall Avenue, then take a left onto Ocean Avenue. Follow Ocean Avenue southwest 1 3/4 miles to the King's Beach Fisherman's Access Parking Area on the left, or continue on Ocean Avenue 1/2 mile to parking areas in Brenton Point State Park.

A rocky shore, crashing surf and a south-facing shoreline add up to a classic location for the surfcaster seeking a trophy bass or bluefish. There is a little more than a mile of shoreline to fish at **Brenton Point**, but this area should be viewed as a spot for the experienced angler only. The smooth, slate-rock formations are covered with slippery seaweed in many places, so be sure to wear studded-soled waders and tread carefully. At times huge ocean swells break over these rocks, another reason to approach the water's edge with caution. The experienced surfhands will watch the water for a few minutes and wait for a set of waves to break, giving them enough information to plan where they can cast and land a fish safely.

This chaotic underwater environment is a fish magnet, though, and more big stripers are taken from shore at this location than anywhere else on Aquidneck Island. Heavy surf gear is the rule, as are big plugs for big fish. Try a surface swimming plug, large wooden poppers or shallow-running lures right in the wash. Eels cast after dark account for some trophy stripers, too. Because of the uneven, rocky bottom and strong currents, this is not a place to attempt bottom fishing. In many cases, there are deep pockets next to the rock formations that are good holding water for large stripers and bluefish. On the northwest side of the point there is a jetty that can be fished at the lower end of the tide if there isn't too big a swell running. The protected water behind the jetty is a preferred spot for fly-rodders looking for schoolie stripers and the occasional bigger fish.

This is another very scenic area and there are picnic areas and

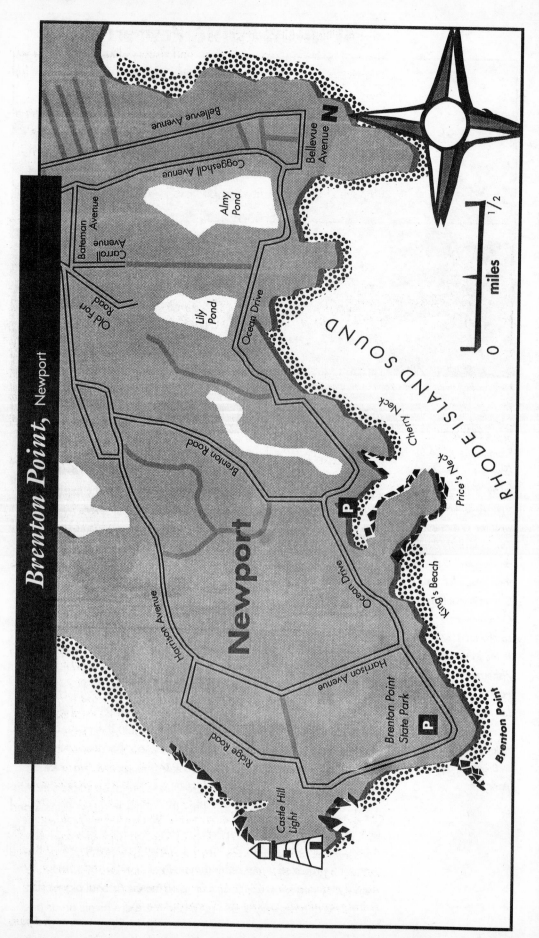

Brenton Point, Newport

other facilities available on the state park grounds across the street. The spot is very popular with locals and visitors alike, so it's important to arrive early or after hours in the summer to find a parking spot, but that's when you'll have the best fishing anyway.

If you do plan to fish after dark, scope the area out carefully in the daytime and consider wearing an inflatable lifevest for safety's sake. And always wear studded-soled waders or the slip-on rubber-soled and steel-spiked creepers. This is a premier location for catching large fish, one of the best in the state, but hardly worth a dunking or worse.

The jetty on the west side of Brenton Point is known as the Rock Pile.

All Summer Long

After one has been surf casting for a while, certain things become clear. In a general sense, dusk and dawn are productive times to fish; it's best to fish at night for large stripers; an onshore wind creates favorable surf conditions. The list goes on and on. There are certain negative generalities also. Probably the most basic one being, day fishing in the summer is slow. Every rule has its exceptions however, and Brenton Point is the exception.

For some reason, and I do not know what it is, people catch fish from shore, stripers and blues mind you, in the middle of the day, in the summer, at Brenton Point. Day fishing in the summer for stripers and blues is almost unheard of just about everywhere. What is even more amazing is what the fish hit: popping plugs. I would be less surprised if I heard that chunkers fishing a hole did well in daylight, or that fish were jigged up from the bottom with the sun high in the sky—they probably are on occasion—but poppers are, by far, the preferred daytime method here. This is not to say that daytime summer fishing at Brenton Point is the best time and season, but Brenton produces at a time when others simply do not.

I do know that the waters around Jamestown and Newport are fairly deep and therefore, slow to warm. Even on a hot June day in the city, it is often brisk in the City By The Sea. Just stick your head out the window the next time you are going over the Pell Bridge on a hot day and you will get a first-hand confirmation. The cooler, deeper water surrounding the island often results in the summer's fishing doldrums passing the Newport area by.

J. Lyons

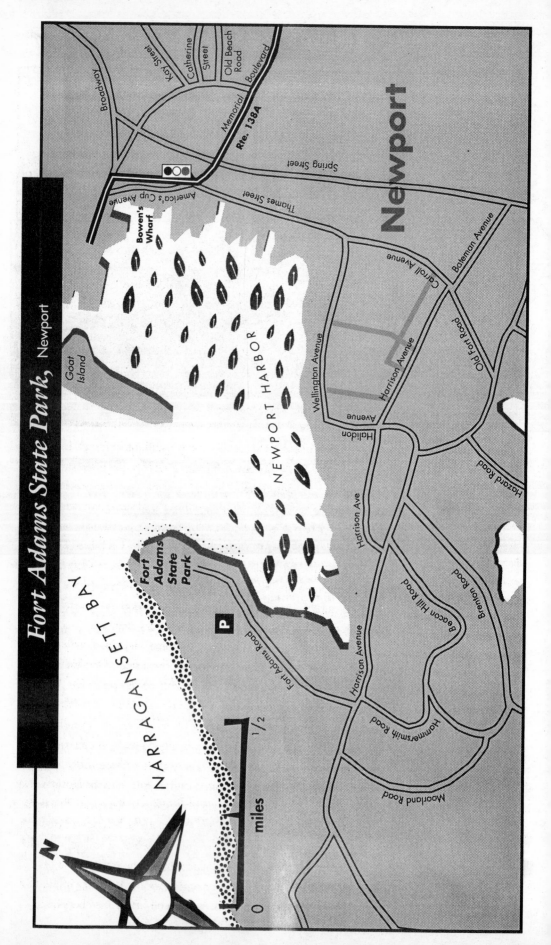

Fort Adams State Park, Newport

Fort Adams State Park, Newport

Stripers, bluefish and tautog are found along the west side of Fort Adams State Park.

Directions:

From Route 138A in downtown Newport at Bowen's Wharf, follow Thames Street south 3/4 mile to Old Fort Road. Continue southwest on Old Fort Road for 1/8 mile to Harrison Avenue on the right. Follow Harrison Avenue 1 1/8 miles to the state park entrance on the right. Follow the park access road 1/2 mile to the parking area.

Certainly one of the most scenic fishing locations in Rhode Island, the grounds of the **Fort Adams State Park** are a great family fishing and picnic destination. The fort, which was constructed in stages between 1820 and 1853, was one of the most formidable and important coastal defense installations on the East Coast of the United States in the nineteenth century. During the Civil War the US Naval Academy was located inside its walls and it remained an active military base until the state took over in 1965. Today it is used by everyone from school athletic groups to joggers to picnicing families, and the annual Newport Folk and Jazz Festivals are held here every summer.

Local fishermen come here, too, for some very good early and late season flounder fishing along the east (harbor) side of the facility and good striper and bluefishing all season long on the west side. At the southern end of the grounds are docks and a lagoon area that is a good early season tautog spot and holds fluke later on. If you're seeking stripers or blues, try working along the rocky shores on the west side of the point. Deep water is very close to these rocky formations and long casts are not required and, in fact, may be less effective than working a swimming plug, eel or fly close to the rocks. First light or evening fishing is best, after harbor boat traffic has slowed down.

With acres of green lawns down to the water, a sailing museum and interpretive center on the grounds, restroom facilities, the constant activity of the nearby harbor and brooding presence of the fort itself, this is a wonderful location to keep all family members happy for an afternoon or evening outing.

What Fishing Reports Mean

Some people criticize published fishing reports as being week-old information, or worse, misinformation. While the former is true, anyone believing the later is usually also tossing around some colorful conspiracy theories. Reports are most valuable when the fish are in residency, roughly June through September. In Rhode Island the fishing can remain good at certain places for long periods. And, if you save the reports, as many do, or read past reports at the local library, trends appear. If the variables between years are similar, one can sometimes predict the future with reasonable certainty.

From Fort Adams, the view north includes the Newport Bridge.

Reading the reports and noticing the trends is one of the first steps an angler takes to become a more sophisticated fisherman. Later you'll be able to read between the lines, and if you do not see certain places mentioned, alongside the ones that are, it usually means the quiet guys are fishing there. Conspicuous omissions become highly suspect. While Rhode Island is a great surfcaster's state, catching fish from shore is difficult at certain times of the season. The best surfcasters make use of any and all information available to them.

One of the most reliable trends is that surfcasting success in the Newport area picks up just as the Bay slows down due to rising water temperatures. Each year, usually during mid to late June, the action shifts from the mid Bay to lower Bay. By mid to late July, when the bottom has fallen out for some, Iron Mike or someone like him fishing Newport, appears in a fishing report with a 40. You can count on it.

After a long while, you will be able to predict the upcoming fishing report with a fairly high degree of accuracy. Fishing for stripers becomes a predictable hopscotch all around the state. The level of sophistication, particularly among those who aren't talking, is amazing. One guy actually picked up on the fact that I had done well at a certain spot because he found, in his words, "a scale." From that one scale, which he found at night, he was able to determine the fish's size and where I had been casting.

J. Lyons

Goat Island Causeway, Newport

Directions:

Follow Route 138A (Memorial Boulevard) in downtown Newport southwest to the waterfront area. At the traffic lights at the bottom of the hill near

This area is tailor-made for bottom-fishing enthusiasts. Along with a great place to get a bunch of scup with the kids, more serious bottom dunkers come here for fluke and blackfish. The fluke start to show right around the end of May, and the blackfish will be here both in the spring and again in the fall. **Goat Island Causeway** is not strictly a bait-fishing spot, however. In the spring and early summer, tinker mackerel are caught here on light tackle. From the spring right through the summer the causeway is often lined from nightfall to dawn

Bottom fishermen like the east side wall at Fort Adams.

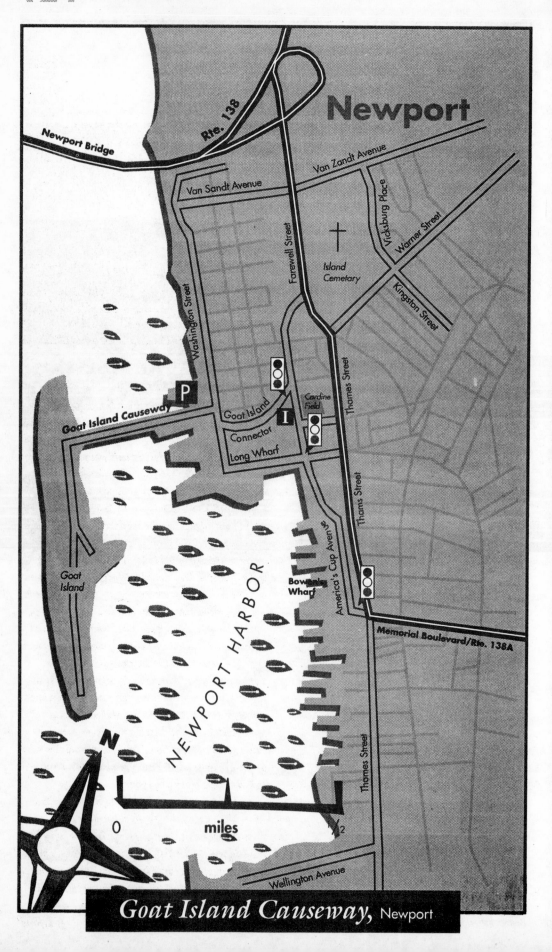

Goat Island Causeway, Newport

A young fisherman tries his luck next to the Goat Island Causeway.

Bowen's Wharf, turn right onto America's Cup Avenue. Follow America's Cup Avenue north 0.3 mile past the Visitor's Center to Goat Island Connector on the left. Follow Goat Island Connector 0.3 mile west to the causeway. Park along the causeway in the designated parking lane.

with folks jigging squid, which are attracted to the lights that line the bridge. Sometimes in the late summer and early fall false albacore are even caught as they charge around the inner Newport Harbor area.

Fishing the causeway will never be confused with the wide-open surf-casting experience of Brenton or Sachuest points. But for youngsters, older anglers who may be wary of slippery rocks and crashing surf, or anyone looking for a good fishing location with easy access, this may be the perfect spot. If the causeway gets crowded, nearby stone piers just to the north are good alternatives.

Squid Country

Call it squid or call it calamari, but fishing for this mollusk to use as bait, to stuff, or to fry has been popular for some time, and the Goat Island Causeway is one of the best places in the state to find it. Each year, around the first week of May, armed with squid jigs and five-gallon buckets for filling (and they do fill them!), squid fishers arrive at the causeway.

The requirements for catching squid are fairly simple. You need darkness, artificial lights to attract the squid, a pole and a squid jig. The best lures for catching squid are Japanese "bird" models. Tackle dealers and fishermen usually agree that pink is the best color, followed by white. Squid are not a great challenge to catch; it is more harvest than sport. Moon tides (tides around the new or full moons) increase the abundance of squid in Newport Harbor.

As the month progresses from early to late May, the desirable (from a human consumption standpoint), smaller squid give way to the bigger specimens, and where there is bait, there are gamefish. The arrival of squid on Aquidneck Island triggers, in earnest, the start of striper season.

J. Lyons

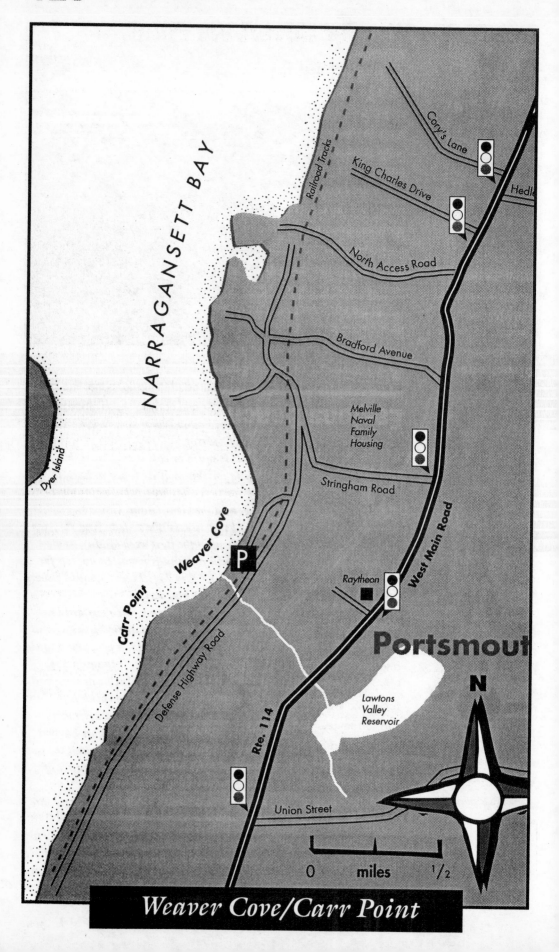

NARRAGANSETT BAY

Dyer Island

Railroad Tracks

Cory's Lane

King Charles Drive

Hedle

North Access Road

Bradford Avenue

Melville
Naval
Family
Housing

Stringham Road

West Main Road

Carr Point

Weaver Cove

P

Raytheon

Portsmout

Defense Highway Road

Rte. 114

Lawtons
Valley
Reservoir

N

Union Street

0   miles   1/2

Weaver Cove/Carr Point

Weaver Cove/Carr Point,
Portsmouth

The beach at Weaver Cove curves toward Carr Point.

Directions:
From Route 114 in Portsmouth, follow Stringham Road west 0.5 mile, then north 0.25 mile to Defense Highway. Turn south (a hard left) onto Defense Highway and follow for 0.5 mile to the access road on the right, to Weaver Cove boat launch and parking area.

Good access, plenty of parking and a location where bait fishermen and light-tackle enthusiasts can find success makes **Weaver Cove** popular throughout the fishing season. Years ago when winter flounder were plentiful, this was a well-known spot with the flatfish fraternity. Now that winter flounder are beginning to make a modest comeback, Weaver Cove may just be the place to drown a few sandworms during those first few warm days in March. Blackfish (tautog) fans catch plenty of fish here, too.

As spring moves into summer, fly-rodders show up here to tangle with schoolie stripers and bluefish. The southern end of the cove, **Carr Point**, is a good place to fish chunk bait when the pogies start to move around Narragansett Bay, and it's also popular with pluggers. There is plenty of room to spread out along the beach for bottom fishing, and most fishermen prefer the top of the tide to halfway into the ebb. Stripers chase silversides here at night throughout the season, often right along the beach, so light-tackle anglers fishing small jigs and small soft rubber baits do very well.

An Untouched Sanctuary
Directly across from Weaver Cove you'll notice a small island. This is Dyer Island, a parcel of roughly 28 acres that has recently been purchased by the state and will be

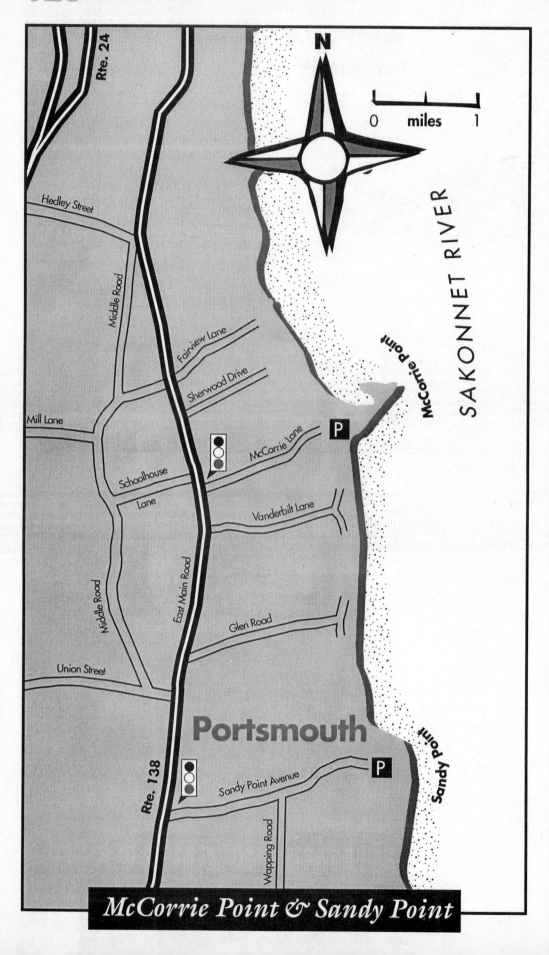

McCorrie Point & Sandy Point

added to the Narragansett Bay National Estuarine Research Reserve.

The island has a peak elevation of just 13 feet and becomes completely submerged during hurricanes. One of the very few untouched salt marshes in Narragansett Bay, Dyer Island is also one of the few sites in the state that is home to nesting oyster catchers, one of the state's rarest shorebirds. The purchase was made principally for research. The pristine salt marsh will serve as a model for the Department of Environmental Management's salt marsh restoration projects.

According to Roger Greene, DEM manager of the Narragansett Bay reserve, Dyer Island will be open to boaters and kayakers. The Narragansett Bay reserve is one in a national system of 25 estuarine reserves, protecting more than one million acres of upland, freshwater wetland, salt marshes, inter-tidal areas and subtidal areas.

J. Lyons

McCorrie Point, Portsmouth

The Sakonnet River is east of McCorrie Point.

Directions:

From Route 138 in Portsmouth, follow McCorrie Point Lane northeast 1 mile to the beach.

Located on the western shore of the Sakonnet River, **McCorrie Point** is popular with local anglers because there is adequate parking, good water movement to deliver plenty of bait for the stripers and bluefish that can be found nearby all season long, and room to spread out. Flounder and tautog can be taken off the southeast corner of the point in the spring and again in the fall. Off the outermost part of the point is a sandbar that fly and light-tackle enthusiasts like to wade and fish. Another plan is to walk and cast along the shore, working south toward Sandy Point, another good fishing location. This shoreline has a sloping rocky bottom with plenty of weeds and cover for striped bass. Casting live eels here after dark produces large stripers every year.

A Family Fish Feed

There are many types of fishing that go on at McCorrie Point, but the most productive seems to be scup fishing. The numbers of scup available at McCorrie Point appear to be limitless. I'm not a scup fisherman, but I've observed families fishing here in preparation for a fish fry and marveled at their systematic approach.

Fancy surf-fishing gear is not necessary. The typical scup rig is a bottom-fishing rod and reel equipped with a number 2 hook, as the scup's mouth is small, and a 2-ounce sinker. The hook should be on a fairly short leader of about 12 to 18 inches, sweetened with small pieces of worm or squid. The offering is then cast and allowed to sink to the bottom. The angler then lowers the rod and gives the tip a series of little jerks.

Slack tide is the best time to go for scup, and remember, they have spiked dorsal fins, so when handling, be sure to push the fins down toward the tail to avoid a puncture wound.

It does not take long to catch scup when they are around, which is usually from May through September. In short order, I've seen families catch enough fish for six people. The men and kids hand the fish to the mom, who fillets faster than I thought possible. People still fish for food, however unstylish it may be to sport-fishing purists. Scup is as delicious a fish as you are likely to catch.

J. Lyons

Sandy Point, Portsmouth

Directions:
From Route 138 in Portsmouth, go east on Sandy Point Road 1 1/4 miles to the beach.

Although access to the beach parking area can be a problem at the height of the summer season (the gate is sometimes locked at night), this area is well worth checking out. Local anglers prefer a southeast breeze and a falling tide at first light or in the evening when stripers and bluefish will sometimes push silversides or menhaden right up to the edge of the beach. There is a deep drop-off very close to shore here into the Sakonnet River and the nighttime chunk-bait fishing can be very productive. To the south of the point and the sandy beach the sand and gravel bottom gives way to large boulders and weed patches. Walk and cast along this shore with slow-swimming surface plugs or live eels after dark. This 1 1/2-mile stretch of shoreline running south to Black Point has also been the scene of some good false albacore fishing in recent years.

A Sweet Spot
Sandy Point is one of those chameleon spots, sometimes bathing beach, sometimes birdwatchers outpost and sometimes a striper fisherman's hot spot. It depends on when you catch it. Sandy Point's gates close at 9 P.M., so night fishing is not a viable option.

Sandy Point is about as physically undemanding a fishing spot as you will find—no cliffs to climb down, no long hikes from the parking lot. It is a good place to introduce a child to saltwater fishing, particularly at dusk or when skipjack bluefish are known to

A flock of brants enjoys low tide off Sandy Point.

be about. The cooperative bluefish will keep the little ones, and their short attention spans, happily occupied. The best time to fish for bass, blues or scup at Sandy Point is roughly an hour before sunset, continuing into twilight.

Success on their first outings seems to be the trick to getting kids interested in fishing. In short, kids like to catch. This means going when the fish are most likely to bite, not when it is most convenient for the instructor. A child who stands in the hot sun for two hours without so much as a tap is most likely going to bring the handheld video game the next time someone suggests fishing.

For those who like to bait fish there are good numbers of scup. A small hook, sweetened with clamworm on a short leader in conjunction with a 2-ounce sinker, works well. Any of the local tackle shops will happily provide advice on rigging up and what is running.

Sandy Point is a lovely spot for a late-afternoon picnic followed by some fishing. The spot affords some panoramic vistas of the Sakonnet with room to walk and explore for those not interested in fishing. The Town of Portsmouth allows sportsmen to use this facility, so don't leave any trash or monofilament behind.

There is one serious concern for anyone who takes his or her children to Portsmouth to fish on a summer evening. Be advised that a trip down Route 138 will lead an unsuspecting adult past not one, not two, but a gauntlet of the most distracting alternative to fishing: the roadside ice cream shop. It seems like there are more places to purchase an ice cream cone on this road than anywhere else along the striper coast. Don't say you weren't warned!

J. Lyons

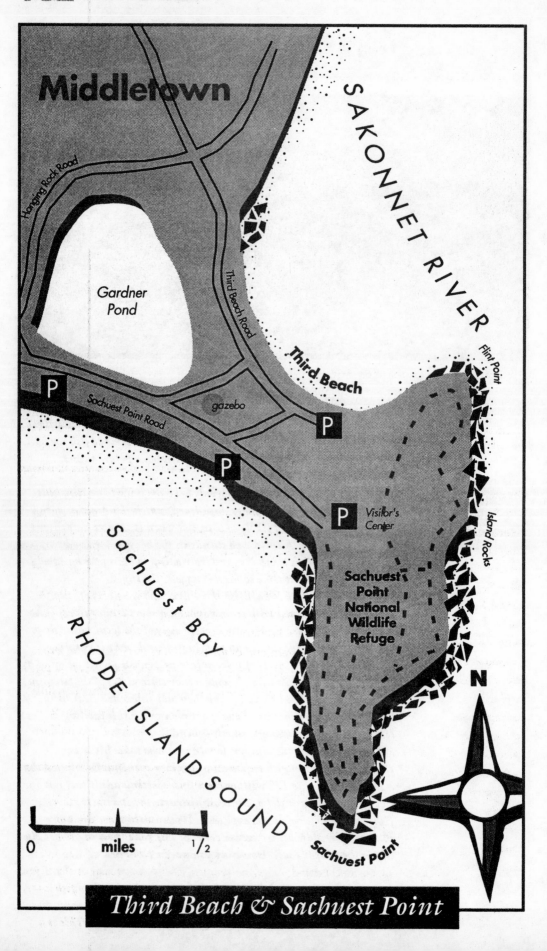

Middletown

SAKONNET RIVER

Hanging Rock Road

Gardner Pond

Third Beach Road

Third Beach

Flint Point

P

Sachuest Point Road

gazebo

P

P

P

Visitor's Center

Sachuest Bay

Island Rocks

Sachuest Point National Wildlife Refuge

RHODE ISLAND SOUND

N

0 miles 1/2

Sachuest Point

Third Beach & Sachuest Point

Third Beach, Middletown

The north end of Third Beach is a great fall bluefish spot.

Directions:
From Route 138A near the east end of Easton's (First) Beach at the Newport town line, follow Purgatory Road east for 1 mile. At the west end of Second Beach, bear right onto Hanging Rock Road. Follow Hanging Rock Road for 0.3 mile, then bear right onto Sachuest Point Road. Follow Sachuest Point Road east for 0.3 mile, then bear left onto Third Beach Road. Follow Third Beach Road 0.25 mile to the parking area.

Although fish can be caught here all season long, in the last few years **Third Beach** has really come alive for the fishermen in the late summer and fall with the arrival of huge schools of baby bunker. Stripers and bluefish chase the baitfish into this bay behind the Sachuest Point National Wildlife Refuge area, setting up some spectacular topwater fishing action. The gradual, sloping sand and gravel bottom is also ideal for bait fishing in the early morning or in the evening after the bathers leave the beach.

Toward the eastern end of the beach, there is more rocky structure and some very good striped bass water leading out to Flint Point on Sachuest, where a nice little rip sets up during the incoming tide. In the middle of the beach a small stream flows into the Sakonnet River. This is a favorite spot to fly-fish as the tide drops and baitfish are swept out. Fly-fishermen also appreciate the fact that the prevailing southwest wind is blocked somewhat by the land behind them as they cast and fish.

Out of the Wind and Waves
Third Beach faces the Sakonnet River and, as such, is more sheltered than First or Second beaches. The water here is calmer and sometimes when the other beaches are socked in with weed, Third Beach may be clear. Before deciding on which beach to fish later, take your significant other for a romantic walk along the shore at low tide. This is a

great way to explore the shore while appearing romantic. When you see a bowl or a hole, line the spot up with some landmark and make a mental note for later.

If you are here for a short stay in July or August and want to fish Newport's beaches, here's a tip: Get up early and try gray dawn, or stay up late and fish the deep night. If anything is going to happen in summer, it will happen in the deep night or at first light.

J. Lyons

Sachuest Point, Middletown

Rocky outcroppings and coves line the east side of Sachuest Point.

Directions:

From Route 138A near the east end of Eastons (First) Beach at the Newport town line, follow Purgatory Road east for 1 mile. At the west end of Second Beach, bear right onto Hanging Rock Road. Follow Hanging Rock Road for 0.3 mile, bear right onto Sachuest Point Road and follow for 0.75 mile to the parking area.

Many locals consider **Sachuest Point** the premier shore-fishing spot on Aquidneck Island. The point is a wildlife refuge area with well-maintained grassy trails leading to a number of good fishing spots. The walk from the parking area to the end of the point is about 1/2 mile.

The west side of the point begins at the end of Third Beach and is a great spot to wade and fly-fish if the surf isn't running too high. A little farther out on this western shore is a rocky outcropping that is very popular with the bait-fishing crowd, but care should be taken here also if the surf is high. Stripers, bluefish, blackfish (tautog) and big scup are taken here. At the end of the point you'll find very slippery weed-covered rocks, but by carefully picking your way down to the water's edge and casting surface plugs, you have a good chance to take some large stripers and bluefish.

A path follows the southeastern edge of the point and there are many places to cast among the boulders. This is striper and bluefish country and casting live eels at first light in the fall produces memorable fish every year. The entire east side of the point is fishy water all the way to Flint Point on the northeast end. About halfway down this shore are a group of reefs and small rock formations just offshore, known as Island Rocks. Between them and the shore is a great spot to fish crabs on the bottom for blackfish.

One of the most appealing parts of fishing Sachuest is the setting, a wild, brush-covered expanse that is the most southeasterly point on Aquidneck Island. It is a beautiful place with picnic tables, restroom facilities, which are open during the day in the summer, and several strategically placed benches and observation decks to take in the view. To the east, across the end of the Sakonnet River, is Little Compton and its lighthouse. To the west you can see for miles toward the mansions that line Newport's Cliff Walk. And due south is the open expanse of the Atlantic. This is a wonderful place to take a family for a day of fishing, picnicing and exploring.

Special note should be made, however, of the potentially dangerous fishing conditions here. An angler was killed here when he lost his footing on the seaweed-covered rocks, fell into the churning white water and drowned. This is no place to fish without careful observation of the wash caused by the surf. Always wear studded-soled waders or boots. One of the new self-inflating personal floatation devices is a good idea, too, and could be a lifesaver if you have the misfortune to fall in. This spot fishes best after dark in the middle of the fishing season, but scouting out a safe perch in the daylight is a necessity.

Shockers for Added Protection

Most experienced shore fishermen who fish in rocky areas tie shockers or shock leaders to the end of their lines. A shocker is a heavy piece of line that adds an element of protection against break-offs caused by hooked fish that rub the line against rocks. The shocker should be about the length of your rod, and it should test out at about double the pound test of your running line. The shocker is attached to the running line with a Surgeon's Loop or knot. Make sure you clip the tag ends of the line that form the knot closely, since the knot that holds the shocker to the line must pass through the guides easily when casting. It is especially important to use shockers when fishing in rocky areas with light to medium tackle, along with running lines of 20-pound-test and under.

D. Pickering

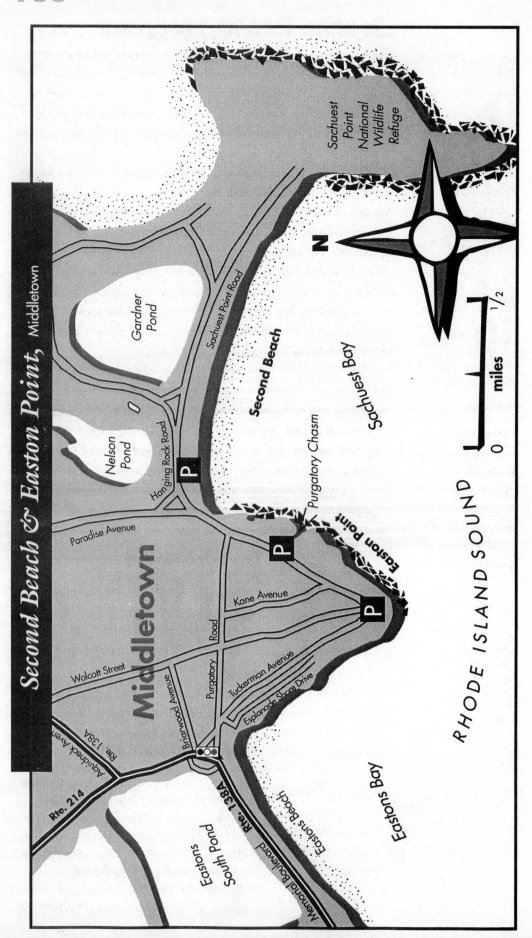

Second Beach & Easton Point, Middletown

Sachuest Point National Wildlife Refuge

N

½

0

miles

Gardner Pond

Sachuest Point Road

Second Beach

Sachuest Bay

Nelson Pond

Hanging Rock Road

Purgatory Chasm

Paradise Avenue

Easton Point

Middletown

Kane Avenue

RHODE ISLAND SOUND

Purgatory Road

Wolcott Street

Tuckerman Avenue

Esplanade Shore Drive

Eastons Bay

Briarwood Avenue

Aquidneck Avenue

Rte. 138A

Rte. 214

Rte. 138A

Memorial Boulevard

Eastons Beach

Eastons South Pond

P

Second Beach, Middletown

To the east along Second Beach is over a mile of good surf-casting water.

Directions:

From the intersection of Route 138A and Purgatory Road, follow Purgatory Road for 1 mile, over the hill to the parking area at the beach.

This is a far better surf-fishing spot in the traditional sense than First Beach (Eastons) only a mile or so away. Armed with a bag of lures and a surf rod, you can walk and plug the length of the beach, with the best fishing taking place at first light and after dark. For some reason, the red seaweed that virtually closes down the fishing in the summer at First Beach is usually confined to a small area of **Second Beach**, near the west end rocks. Fish anywhere else along this beachfront in the early season for schoolies and in the summer (after dark) for larger stripers. This is also a very good place to bottom fish for fluke if the surf isn't running too high. The southwest wind tends to push bait into the eastern corner of the beach where the rocks of Sachuest Point begin, and most locals consider this the best fishing location.

In the last few years huge schools of baby bunker (menhaden) have been trapped in this corner by a combination of strong southwest winds, waves and currents, with certain attack by marauding blues, stripers and sometimes albies the result. This has happened periodically throughout the late summer and fall, and when it has, the fishing has been spectacular.

Early Season, All Season

Second beach is mainly known as the first place stripers show on Aquidneck Island. Around the middle of April, give or take a few days, depending on the severity of the winter, the rumors start flying of school fish, usually in the 12- to 15-inch range, crashing small bucktails and Clouser Minnows. By the end of the month, and well into May, the action is consistent and usually occurs around dusk.

As with many early season spots, Second Beach sometimes gets pigeonholed as an early season spot only. Trying to peg it is about as unfortunate an underestimation as a fisherman can make. Second Beach puts on a different face for almost every month. The Newport regulars know this and keep Second Beach honest by including it in their well-practiced routines.

In the late fall of 2000, anglers were cashing in on highly aggressive, migratory stripers in the 24- to 27-inch range. The fish were feeding on "more bait than you could imagine" and it was like "fishing in a barrel," according to one enthusiastic angler. Many of the participants were fly-fishing or using light tackle. Then, around dusk on September 27, a surfcaster using a large Atom popper hooked and landed a 32-pound bass. The large fish dwarfed all the others taken during that blitz.

Was the catch an anomaly, or was the catch a result of an angler's refusal to follow the crowd? As is so often the case, the angler pursuing the large fish caught one.

J. Lyons

Easton Point, Middletown

Directions:
From downtown Newport, follow Route 138A (Memorial Boulevard) 1 1/2 miles northeast (past Eastons Beach). Where Route 138A turns left (north), continue straight on Purgatory Road for 1/8 mile. Turn right onto Tuckerman Avenue. Follow Tuckerman Avenue south for 3/4 mile to the small parking area on the right side of the street. Walk down the path (public right-of-way) to the water.

Similar to Brenton Point to the east but much smaller, **Easton Point** is a classic Rhody rock-ledge/big-surf location. Although there isn't as much room to spread out here as at Brenton, the fishing can be just as good. Some locals feel that the large reef just offshore attracts striped bass and bluefish, and those fish will also cruise the nearby shore. Wooden swimming plugs and poppers work here, and this is a favorite spot to cast live eels into the breakers. Be very careful walking on the weed-covered rocks.

Look To The Point

There's something about a point that sets a surfcaster's heart to racing. And if there isn't, there should be. Points are perennial hot spots. When I was a young surfcaster, I used to fish a cove, nearby this one, with marginal success. I would walk along, fanning out my casts, swimming plugs at night. I thought I knew what I was I doing, catching school bass and sometimes a big bluefish. I was in that transitional period many fishermen go through, when fishing success starts to overshadow failure.

I think it was my fourth of fifth year of surfcasting when I found a new fishing buddy. He was older than me by maybe 15 years and educated at the University of Narragansett. He was one of those rabid surfcasters you hear about. He had been mentored by another surfcaster, one who traced his lineage back to the post-war advent of surfcasting. My new friend was

Easton Point offers classic striped bass water.

old school: willing to walk a long way, go without sleep, endure cold, anything for the prospect of a "good fish." I could not believe my good fortune when I met him.

When spring rolled around we started fishing, though not immediately together. He had been out "prospecting" on his own, hitting a variety of spots, trying to get a pulse on where the fish were. He had not found any significant concentration, but I had been getting fish in my cove, so I suggested we go there. I added that they were mainly schoolies, and not to expect anything too big.

We arrived at the cove and I confidently started my little routine with my swimming plug and he, silently, fished alongside. After we had caught a few school fish, he suggested we go around the cove, up to a little point, maybe a 1/4 mile south. Once we arrived and set up, he looked at the water, made a cast to the side of the point the tide was flowing from, then hooked and landed a fish of 20 pounds—then another, then another and then a fourth.

I had been fishing the cove for years and never caught a keeper there, his first night in a new spot and he caught four! It was my first basic surfcasting lesson: Fish the points for big, opportunistic stripers. I had read about structure and its influence on water flow, but I was so excited with my own limited success that I had failed to look deeper—until the night I was shown.

J. Lyons

Purgatory Chasm is a break in the rocks that line Easton Point.

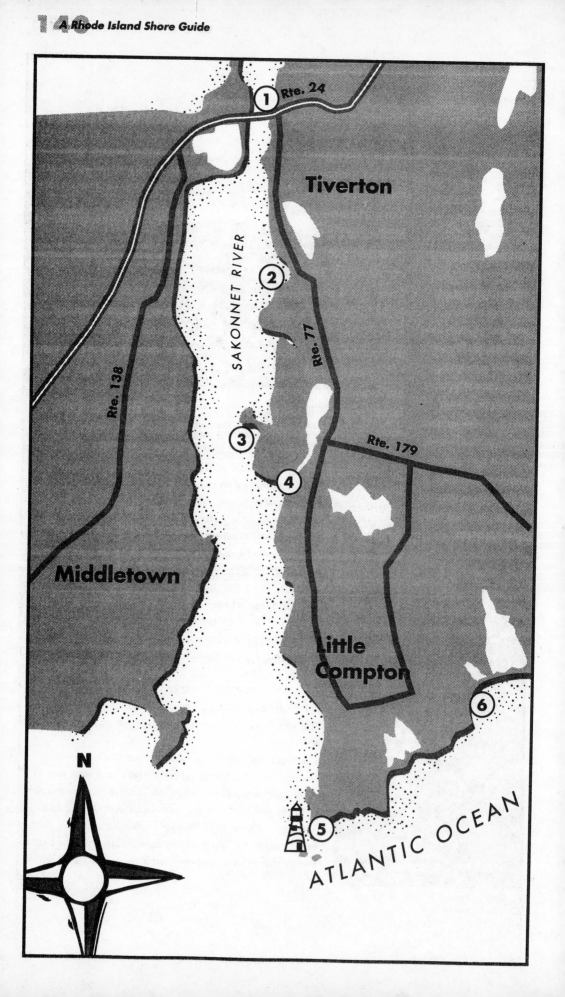

Rte. 24

Tiverton

Sakonnet River

Rte. 77

Rte. 138

Rte. 179

Middletown

Little Compton

N

ATLANTIC OCEAN

Eastern Rhode Island

Exploring and fishing the eastern shore of the Sakonnet River in the towns of Tiverton and Little Compton is, in some ways, like stepping back in time. Working farms, orchards and vineyards stretch all the way to the water's edge in many places. At the end of coastal Route 77 is Little Compton Harbor, shared by recreational and commercial fishing boats. This part of Rhode Island has for the most part escaped commercial development and looks much the same as it did a hundred years ago. Tourists who look out at the rocky outcroppings around West Island and Sakonnet Light see a picture-postcard image of coastal New England, but fishermen see reefs, shoals and rips that hold big striped bass and bluefish.

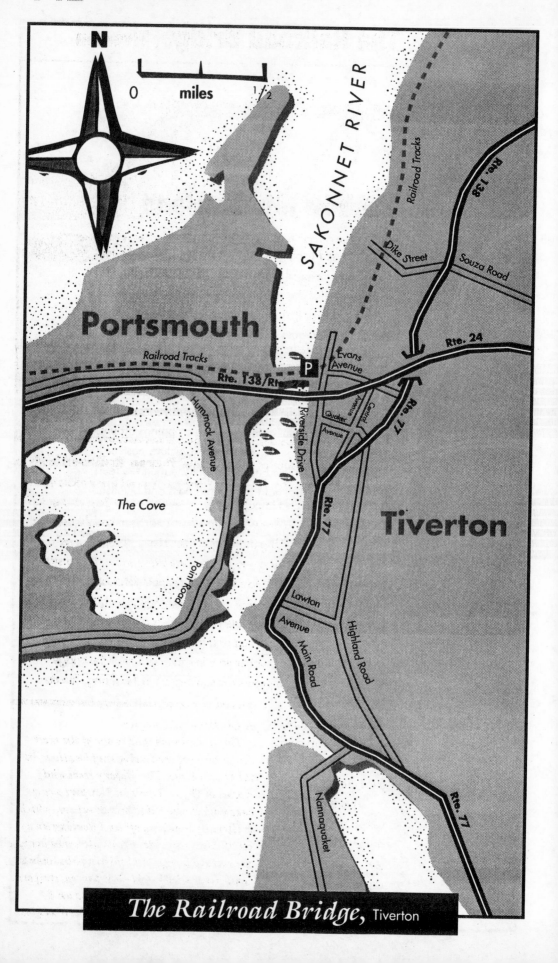

N

0 miles 1/2

SAKONNET RIVER

Railroad Tracks

Rte. 138

Dike Street

Souza Road

Portsmouth

Railroad Tracks

Rte. 24

P

Evans Avenue

Rte. 138/Rte. 24

Rte. 77

Quaker Avenue

Central Avenue

Riverside Drive

Hummock Avenue

Rte. 77

Tiverton

The Cove

Point Road

Lawton Avenue

Main Road

Highland Road

Nannaquaket

Rte. 77

The Railroad Bridge, Tiverton

The Railroad Bridge, Tiverton

The old railroad trestle no longer completely spans the Sakonnet River.

Directions:

From Route 24 south, take the Tiverton exit. Turn left onto Route 77. Follow Route 77 south for 1/2 mile to the first right, Riverside Avenue. Follow Riverside Avenue north along the waterfront for 1/2 mile to the trestle.

This abandoned spur of the old **New Haven Railroad** leads to the rocky footings and riprap of a bridge. Around these rocks you'll find some of the best tautog fishing in Narragansett Bay, and in the past few seasons, a few winter flounder have been caught here too. This spot has everything that tautog like: plenty of rocky cover and weedbeds; crabs, clams and musselbeds everywhere; plus a strong current due to the constriction of the Sakonnet River at this point.

The tautog fishing is best in April and May and again in October and November, when the water cools. This is also a good nighttime spot to cast a swimming plug or a live eel at in the summer months for stripers. A bucktail or rubber jig allowed to sink near the bridge abutments could also produce a squeteague in the spring. The challenge with any of these larger gamefish is to keep them away from the structure once they're hooked.

This is a thickly settled residential area, so be sure to respect property rights and park in designated areas only.

A Challenging Location

This abandoned spur is one of the most dangerous yet productive surf locations in the Ocean State. The slippery rocks and washes of Ocean Drive in Newport are a cakewalk compared to this structure, which is literally breaking off and floating away on almost every tide. The anglers who brave the rotting pilings and shifting abutments come away with world-class tautog, stripers and bluefish, and weakfish up to an 8-pound, 8-ounce specimen have been weighed

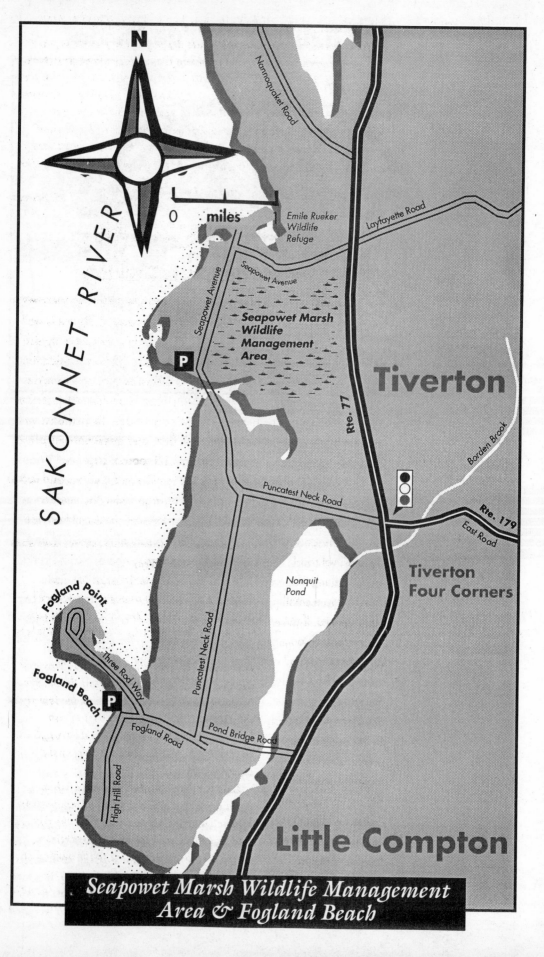

Nannaquaket Road

Layfayette Road

Emile Rueker
Wildlife
Refuge

Seapowet Avenue

Seapowet Avenue

**Seapowet Marsh
Wildlife
Management
Area**

P

Tiverton

Rte. 77

Borden Brook

Rte. 179

Puncatest Neck Road

East Road

Nonquit
Pond

**Tiverton
Four Corners**

Fogland Point

Puncatest Neck Road

Three Rod Way

Fogland Beach

P

Fogland Road

Pond Bridge Road

High Hill Road

Little Compton

S A K O N N E T   R I V E R

N

0   miles

**Seapowet Marsh Wildlife Management
Area & Fogland Beach**

in at the bait shop located a short distance east of the spur.

One fisherman, who rows his 8-foot dinghy to the pilings to gain access to the great spring tautog fishing from the swaying structure, says that it is like hang gliding with a rod and reel. Access from the Portsmouth side of the spur is more difficult, but the footing is much better, if you call standing on a slab of granite 15 feet above a roaring current "better." Bass to 42 pounds have been bucktailed from the structure, and many larger fish have been lost when they head for the safety of the pilings and cut off 80-pound-test mono like so much soft twine.

C. Soares

Seapowet Marsh Wildlife Management Area, Tiverton

Directions:

From Tiverton center, drive south 3 miles on Route 77 to Seapowet Road on the right. Follow Seapowet Road west for 0.7 mile, then south for 0.7 mile. The parking area is next to the bridge.

Seapowet Marsh Wildlife Management Area is well known by waterfowlers, but the marsh is also a prime spot to fly-fish for stripers and weakfish. Wade carefully along the banks inside the bridge on the south side and you'll find schoolies chasing silversides almost every night from July through October. High tide and just after the turn is when you want to fish outside the bridge. Striped bass will stack up in the channel waiting for this bait, and this is another prime spot to fly-fish at dawn or just after dark all season long.

This is also a popular spot for local families to dig clams, and some fishermen feel that this activity attracts the large tautog that are frequently caught off the beach in the spring and fall. Looking northwest from the bridge you'll see a gravel road running along the shore out to a small parking area. If you decide to drive out, be aware that this road may be submerged during times of extreme high tide. To the north of the point parking area there is a small tidal pond that also dumps bait on a falling tide and is a good spot to look for cruising stripers after dark.

A Great Spot for Weakfish

This is one of the most accessible and productive locations along the east shore of the Sakonnet River. The bridge on the east side of the road transits a vast estuary where baitfish of all sorts thrive and grow to maturity. On an outgoing tide the narrow channel on the northwest side of the bridge holds predators, particularly under low-light conditions. The tides carry bait to fish holding in the Sakonnet from the trough at the bridge to the flat on both sides of the marsh entrance.

Last year we caught three weakfish to 6 pounds while a Rhode Island Conservation officer watched us hook and fight the fish. He told us he had seen numerous weakfish caught from the bridge up to the next creek north of the road where another marsh drains into the Sakonnet. That area is one of the favorite places of the bottom-fishing

Stripers and weakfish can be caught at night inside Seapowet Marsh.

crowd, many of whom like to cast chunks of squid, mackerel and menhaden into the river and catch stripers that work this stretch of the river.

The hardpan beach has always been a favorite launching spot for the shellfishing fleet, which has worked this area for decades. We've launched skiffs and moderate-V boats from the hardpan about 150 yards north of the road. If you use this area for a launching ramp, four-wheel drive is almost a necessity.

C. Soares

Fogland Beach, Tiverton

Directions:

From Tiverton Four Corners go 1 1/4 miles south on Route 77 to Pond Bridge Road on the right. Take a left onto Puncatest Neck Road and a quick right onto Fogland Road. Follow Fogland Road for 1 mile to the beach parking lot. A fee is charged during the day in the summer to park, but there's no fee before or after the beach closes.

A popular spot, **Fogland Beach** is on a peninsula that extends into the Sakonnet River in a beautiful section of the eastern shore of Narragansett Bay. The beachfront on the southwest side drops off quite quickly, making it a good place to bottom fish for flounder and tautog in the early season. Fishermen who like to cast plugs or eels after dark will walk out to the end of the point and cast off the rocks. On the inside of the point is a large shallow area with a firm bottom that is preferred by fly-fishermen and light-tackle enthusiasts.

Stripers and bluefish invade this bay seeking silversides and mummichogs. Because the water is only a few feet deep to well over a hundred yards out from the shore, when these fish are hooked, it's not uncommon for them to make long runs and put on aerial displays. Fogland Beach is also a great place to fish a chunk of herring on the bottom. The nearby herring run into Nonquit Pond is historically one of the most prolific in the state, and it's a good bet that there will be some large stripers nearby when the run is active. Adjacent to the beach is a public boat-launching area and this cove has featured some great false albacore fishing in the late season for the past few years.

Looking south along Fogland beach toward the boat ramp.

Bottom Fishing

This area is also utilized as the Tiverton Town Beach, and early risers and latecomers can fish without paying the charge during the daytime hours. The stretch of shoreline here is one of the most picturesque on the Sakonnet River, and Portsmouth and Middletown, Rhode Island, are just a short distance across this narrow portion of the river. Fogland Point is composed of the shale rock that is common in this part of Rhode Island, and has always been one of the premiere scup and tautog spots for shore-bound anglers. Casting from the point to the west, fishermen catch respectable stripers, blues and weakfish on the uneven bottom that stretches from the shoreline out to the channel. Around the point there is a shallow area that warms up before the rest of the river, providing a haven for baitfish and light-tackle enthusiasts, who work the morning and evening tides here in the spring and fall.

C. Soares

Peckham's Creek/Donovan's Marsh,
Tiverton/Little Compton

Directions:

From the junction of Route 77 and Route 179 in Tiverton, follow Route 77 south 2.1 miles to Town Way Road on the right. Follow Town Way Road down the hill to the water. Limited parking is available at the bottom of the hill.

For generations the waters of **Peckham's Creek** and the surrounding **Donovan's Marsh** area have been a popular destination for fishermen, clammers and waterfowlers. Fishermen come here in the spring for big stripers that are attracted to the herring, which move in on their way to the creek's headwaters, Nonquit Pond. The herring run is one of the most productive in the state, and the well-maintained flume area to net the baitfish is on nearby Pond Bridge Road.

As the marsh floods, stripers move into the upper reaches of the creek. When the tide begins to drop, these fish exit the creek and this is a good time to drift a live herring near the mouth or fish chunk bait

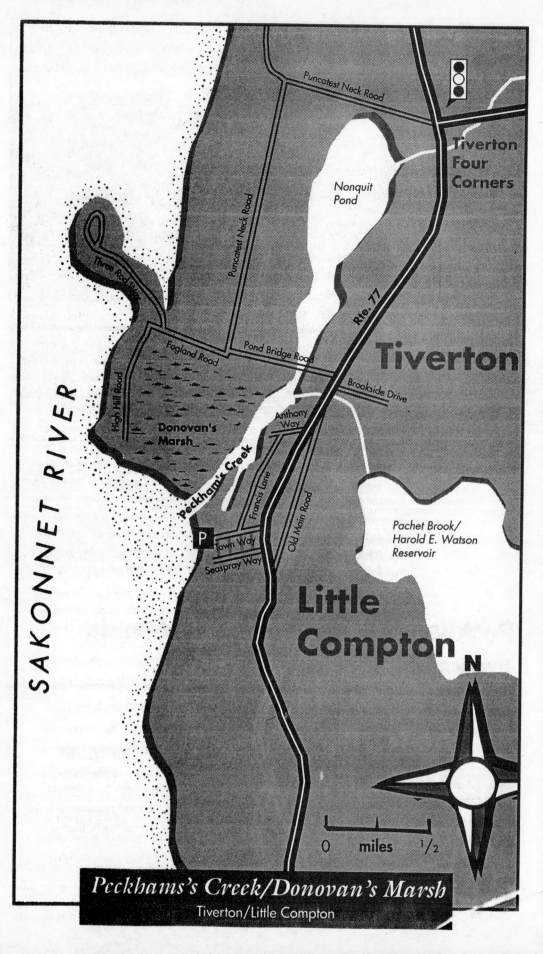

Puncatest Neck Road

Tiverton Four Corners

Nonquit Pond

Puncatest Neck Road

Three Rod Way

Rte. 77

Tiverton

Fogland Road

Pond Bridge Road

High Hill Road

Brookside Drive

Donovan's Marsh

Anthony Way

Peckham's Creek

Francis Lane

Old Main Road

Pachet Brook/ Harold E. Watson Reservoir

P

Town Way

Seaspray Way

Little Compton

SAKONNET RIVER

N

0   miles   1/2

Peckhams's Creek/Donovan's Marsh
Tiverton/Little Compton

all season long. The outflow at the mouth is also a great place to cast flies after dark from July into the fall. Duck hunters report seeing big stripers in the creek right into November, making this a good bet for some late-season action as well.

The entrace to Peckham's Creek is barely visible at low tide.

Ducks and Herring

The creek winds and meanders from the roadway, along a pristine network of ditches and feeders, until it exits into the Sakonnet River. This very popular fishing, claming and waterfowling location has some deep gullies that hold large fish waiting in ambush of herring dropping back on the low tide. We've caught stripers and weakfish, which follow the herring up to the head of the run, holding along the deep edges where egrets and great blue heron feed. Bass to 25 pounds have been caught by fishermen live-lining herring at the mouth where the creek dumps into the Sakonnet. In the early morning a quiet fishermen can see the dorsals of bass holding in the shallow water, waiting for a herring to drop back into the river. Waterfowlers report spooking large bass right up to the early weeks of the November season as they paddle the creek to their blinds.

C. Soares

Sakonnet Point, Little Compton

Directions:

Follow Route 77 south to its end. Park at the public lot adjacent to the seafood packing plant.

Next to the parking area is a long jetty that protects a small harbor that is popular with both commercial fishermen and pleasure boaters. The jetty is a great place to take kids on a summer day for some bottom fishing for scup, tautog or fluke. At night, bottom fishermen seeking stripers take over, fishing cut bait or live eels. Late in the season, false albacore and bonito sometimes sweep along the jetty, offering fast action for anglers set up with light tackle. This is one of

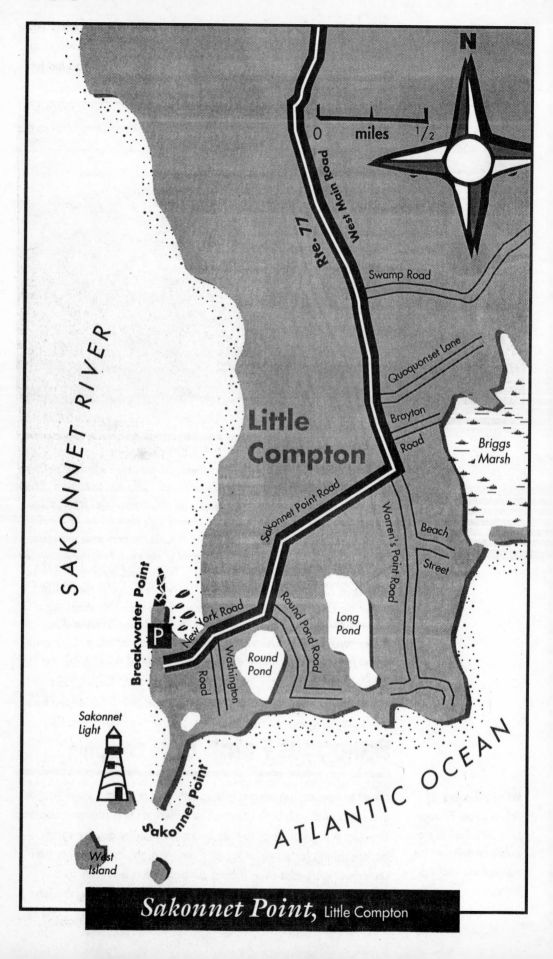

N

0 miles 1/2

Rte. 77

West Main Road

Swamp Road

Quoquonset Lane

Brayton

Road

Briggs Marsh

SAKONNET RIVER

Little Compton

Sakonnet Point Road

Warren's Point Road

Beach

Street

Breakwater Point

P

New York Road

Round Pond Road

Long Pond

Washington

Road

Round Pond

Sakonnet Light

Sakonnet Point

ATLANTIC OCEAN

West Island

Sakonnet Point, Little Compton

the few places that shore-bound fishermen have a decent shot at these fast-moving southern fish.

Without a doubt, **Sakonnet Point** itself is one of the most beautiful places to fish in the Ocean State. Rocky outcroppings, a long sandy beach and a much-photographed lighthouse make this location almost a clichéd vision of the New England coast. Next to the

From Sakonnet Point, Sakonnet Light and the remains of the West Island Club are visible offshore.

small island that is home to the lighthouse is West Island. The rocky pillars that can be seen here are all that remains of one of the most famous fishing clubs in New England, the West Island Club.

Formed in the 1850s by a group of rich industrialists and bankers from New York and Philadelphia, the West Island Club once had a large clubhouse and smaller outbuildings on the island, complete with servants, cooks and groundskeepers. Fishing stands were constructed along the shore for members to fish for striped bass and bluefish. In the 1860s a few members of the West Island Club formed the more famous Cuttyhunk Club on the westernmost of the nearby Elizabeth Islands. The West Island Club flourished until the early part of the twentieth century when striped bass stocks went into a severe and extended decline. The building was burned by vandals in 1929.

What remains today, besides the lonely pillars, is the fantastic striper and bluefishing that club members enjoyed a 150 years ago. Besides West Island, small reefs and other islands are quite close to the shore and the confluence of the Sakonnet River with Rhode Island Sound and the Atlantic Ocean, and combined with the prevailing southwest wind, create prime habitat for predators and bait. This is an area that should be explored thoroughly because there are so many channels, rock piles and drop-offs that may hold fish. Surf fishermen will do best on the west side, as long as the winds haven't pushed too much weed into the beach area. On the opposite side of the narrow beach, light-tackle fans will find a sand and rock bottom with grass patches and plenty of cover for striped bass. This is also a good place to cast live eels after dark.

Where Millionaires Fished

The end of Route 77 is the beginning of one of the wildest and most productive stretches of water in the area. The mouth of the Sakonnet River provides a view of the estates of Newport and Ocean Drive a short distance across the river and scenic vistas of the recently restored Sakonnet Lighthouse. The breakwater protects the small harbor,

These fishermen are staked out at the end of the jetty at Breakwater Point.

From the east side of Sakonnet Point, one can look toward Warren's Point.

which is used by commercial fishermen and pleasure boaters.

This is one of the most popular fishing destinations in the Ocean State. Families park alongside the rock structure and fish the entire breakwater, particularly the north end at the light, catching scup, flounder, fluke, sea bass and the occasional stripers and blues, which push bait onto the structure. Some of the best fishing takes place to the south along this rocky breakwater, but the footing is treacherous.

Moving to the south toward the lighthouse puts you into deeper water and less crowded conditions. Lloyds Beach, which is at the end of the road opposite the breakwater side, is private and routinely patrolled by the Little Compton police. Parking on either side of this well-marked, no-parking area will result in a ticket or two for those who ignore the warning. Fishermen arrive here very early in the morning, park in the fish trap lots, and walk to the end of the south road to cast lures and fish bait on the bottom until the beach opens for the day (in the summer).

At the very end of Lloyds Beach (there is a sign identifying this as the Little Compton Driftway, for residents only) is West Island, site of the first organized striped bass club in New England. The three towers that still stand are visible for great distances and are the remains of the main clubhouse and hotel that once graced this historic site. There were also a series of cottages and outbuildings, including a large garden where they grew their produce. Captains of industry, state and federal politicians, and wealthy businessmen sought refuge and some of the best striped bass fishing along the entire migratory range of the striper's domain on this rugged outpost. Because of a continuing argument about the admittance of women, a group of members left to form the more famous Cuttyhunk Bass Club on the westernmost of the Elizabeth Islands.

C. Soares

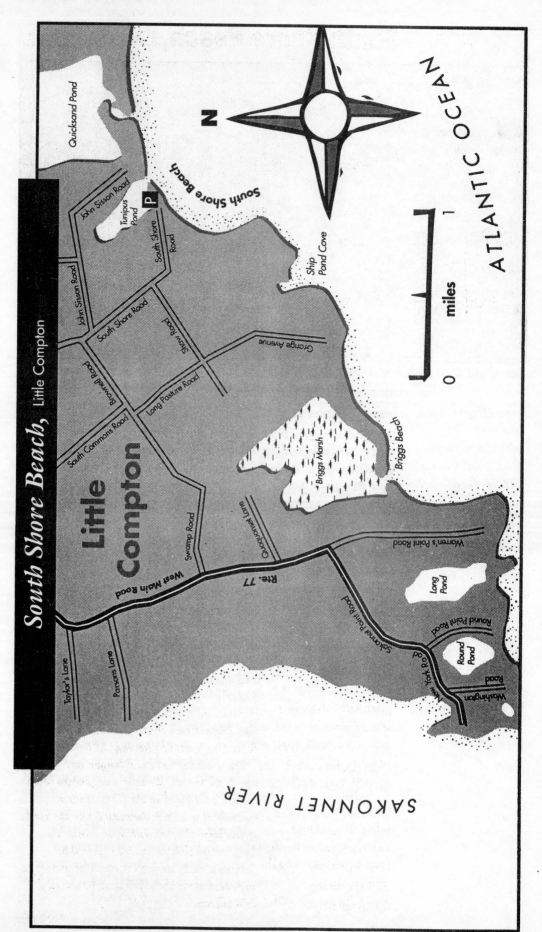

South Shore Beach, Little Compton

South Shore Beach, Little Compton

South Shore Beach provides good shore fishing without a long hike.

Directions:

From Route 77 go 1.7 miles east on Swamp Road, then 1 mile south on South Shore Road to the beach parking area.

A long, sandy public beach on Buzzard's Bay, this shoreline is the easternmost shore area in Rhode Island. **South Shore Beach** is best fished in the early morning or evening when the beach crowd has left for the day, or in the off season. Facing the Bay and the Elizabeth Islands, this is a great location to cast out a chunk of menhaden, herring or a squid strip. Access is easy, there is plenty of parking and the warm waters of the Bay attract early season migrating stripers and bluefish, and fluke and scup in the summer. This is a great location to fish with children or physically challenged anglers who can't walk far from their cars. Late-season surf fishermen can take some large stripers here, especially during a strong southwest blow.

On The State Line

South Shore is a popular and pricey beach spot by day and a fisherman's delight at first light and from evening into the early hours of the morning. There are two herring runs here into Quicksand Pond, the salt pond behind the beach. The first stream is at the end of the parking area and is a very viable herring run that produces herring and a following of stripers and bluefish. Fishermen block off the main course of the stream and allow a trickle to run into the ocean where they chum with cut herring or swim live baits just beyond the breakers.

The second stream is a longer walk, but worth the travel. We have caught bass to 46 pounds and blues in the teens, with an occasional weakfish showing up in the wash. If you have the stamina to continue the walk to Quicksand Point, you will be fishing a rocky area that has been compared with Montauk Point for its productivity and beauty.

C. Soares

Notes:

Notes:

_____

_____

_____

_____

_____

_____

_____

_____

_____

_____

_____

_____

_____

_____

Notes:

Notes:

Notes: